TURBO BLENDER
DESSERT
REVOLUTION

TURBO BLENDER
DESSERT
REVOLUTION

MORE THAN 140 RECIPES FOR
PIES, ICE CREAMS, CAKES, BROWNIES,
GLUTEN-FREE TREATS, AND MORE
FROM HIGH-HORSEPOWER, HIGH-RPM BLENDERS

BRUCE WEINSTEIN & MARK SCARBROUGH
PHOTOGRAPHS BY ERIC MEDSKER

ST. MARTIN'S GRIFFIN
NEW YORK

www.stmartins.com

The Library of Congress Cataloging-in-Publication Data is available upon request.

ISBN 978-1-250-08070-7 (trade paperback)
ISBN 978-1-4668-9260-6 (e-book)

Our books may be purchased in bulk for promotional, educational, or business
use. Please contact your local bookseller or the Macmillan Corporate and
Premium Sales Department at 1-800-221-7945, extension 5442, or by e-mail at
MacmillanSpecialMarkets@macmillan.com.

First Edition: November 2016

10 9 8 7 6 5 4 3 2 1

CONTENTS

A SHORT
INTRODUCTION
TO A
BAKING
REVOLUTION

WELCOME TO A FASTER, EASIER, AND OFTEN BETTER WAY OF MAKING DESSERTS! (HEALTHIER, TOO, IN SOME CASES—BUT WE'LL GET TO THAT.) YOU PROBABLY THOUGHT YOU PURCHASED THAT HIGH-HORSEPOWER, HIGH-RPM BLENDER FOR MAKING ALL SORTS OF SMOOTHIES. YOU MAY HAVE EVEN GONE IN FOR JUICING VEGETABLES TO WHIP UP SNACKS OR ON-THE-GO MEALS. BUT LITTLE DID YOU KNOW WHAT ELSE THAT MACHINE CAN DO! YOU'RE ABOUT TO TURN THAT BLENDER INTO THE BEST TOOL FOR MAKING CREAM PIES, CHEESECAKES, AND GINGERBREAD. YOU'RE ALSO ABOUT TO DISCOVER SOME OF THE MOST EXCITING RECIPES WE'VE EVER CREATED. AND AFTER PUBLISHING OVER 12,000, THAT'S SAYING SOMETHING!

Right up front, let's make sure we're on the same page with the equipment. For these recipes, you need a blender with a high horse-power motor (over 2.0) that spins the blades at high rpms. It must do so fast enough *and* powerfully enough to 1) grind grains and 2) heat soups. The instruction booklet for your machine will highlight both features. We're not talking about standard blenders, or even about high-end blenders sold at specialty kitchenware stores that have high-horsepower motors but fairly standard rpms. These may be able to make flour but they cannot heat liquids by the sheer friction of their blades. If your blender can do both, you're in.

You already know these turbo blenders can grind wheat berries into flour. But that's only half the story. Just add chocolate, butter, sugar, and eggs to that flour *in the canister*, turn the machine on, and you've got a brownie batter in seconds. (Seconds. Literally.) Pour the batter into a pan and bake them up. Then do the same thing for blondies. And scones. And muffins. And sheet cakes. And layer cakes. Now you know why you bought that blender!

Before now, a lot of turbo blender recipes asked you to grind grains in a separate, special canister, then pour the flour into a bowl and continue on making a batter the way you always do, often with an electric mixer in hand. But we don't need a special canister. We don't need an electric mixer. We don't even need another bowl. We'll make most of these desserts in the standard canister, the one that comes with every machine.

Sold? Brownies and layer cakes are just the start! Because the blades spin at a furious rate, we can actually get a custard to its set point in that same canister. Just throw together milk, eggs, and flavorings. Voilà: pudding.

Or a cream pie filling, ready to pour into a graham-cracker crust. Or a panna cotta, that classic Italian dessert. Or just about the creamiest cheesecake around.

And there's still more! Make a slightly thinner custard in the machine, put that covered canister in the fridge, chill the whole thing for a few hours, and pour it into your ice cream maker. Who's up for Butter Pecan? Or Mint Chocolate Chip Ice Cream? Or Cracker Jack? And we haven't even mentioned pancakes and waffles. Or popovers. Or no-bake cheesecakes. Or fruit cobblers. You're going to have that turbo blender out on the counter all the time!

FOUR STEPS TO SUCCESS

STEP 1: FAMILIARIZE YOURSELF WITH YOUR MACHINE.

Yes, we're changing the way you bake. But we won't call for a specific brand of blender. Instead, we'll work across a range. So we need you to commit to a few things. Here are six basic questions you need to answer:

- **How do you operate the various settings?** Know how to turn the machine from high to low speed. In general, we're talking about knowing how to make the blades spin their fastest *and* to make them whir along at a lower, more moderate rate.

- **How can you keep the machine on for as long as you'll need?** Some machines just turn on and off with a switch; others have preset speeds for soups, smoothies, etc. Learn how to override these presets to make the blades spin for as long as the recipe states. In some cases, you need to push the fastest-setting preset button again whenever it times out.

- **How do you pulse the machine on and off?** It's often required in these recipes. Most machines pulse at the highest speed—which is fine for our purposes.

- **Does the lid's center knob have vents at its edge or elsewhere?** In some models, the lid fits securely on the canister without any venting holes or gaps. This will be a problem. You must set that plastic knob askew when things get very hot inside the canister to prevent an explosion of custard across your kitchen. Do not just bump up one corner. Set the knob at a diagonal over the center opening. Or remove the knob entirely and lay a clean kitchen towel over the opening.

- **Does the machine come with a tamper you can insert through the center hole in the lid?** If yours does, you'll use that specially designed tool to help blend thicker doughs and batters. If not, you'll need to resort to a slightly more involved technique: stop the machine repeatedly, scraping down the inside of the canister with a rubber spatula and readjusting the ingredients inside until the batter or dough becomes uniform (or gets to the consistency the recipe indicates). We'll tell you when you need to do what. You must know your options.

- **How do you clean the canister?** For some models, you add water to a specific mark, then add a little liquid detergent before covering and blending at high speed. Others can go straight into the dishwasher.

STEP 2: READ THIS BOOK CAREFULLY.
Since we're inventing a new way to make desserts, there are some subtle and even a few profound changes in the ways these recipes will appear on the page. We've addressed specific concerns in the chapter and section introductions throughout. Don't neglect these! We can't accomplish everything in the headnotes to each recipe. Come prepared.

STEP 3: USE THE RIGHT INGREDIENTS.
Most are standard items in a baker's pantry: chocolate chips, cornstarch, cornmeal, baking soda, and the like. Here are four straight off that need further explanation.

- **Soft white wheat berries.** In almost every recipe that involves baking something in the oven—with the exception of the gluten-free recipes—we call for raw wheat berries. You put them into the blender, grind them into a flour, add the other ingredients, and pour the batter into the pan. Easy enough—except for the part about those wheat berries. In general, wheat berries sold in North America are packaged in two broad categories: either *soft white wheat berries*, sometimes called "spring white" wheat berries; or *hard red wheat berries*, sometimes called "winter red" or just "winter" wheat berries. We only call for the former, the soft white ones. These have a slightly lower protein content than the hard red grains. Soft wheat berries are used in commercial pastry flour; they're also added to cake flour to give baked goods a finer texture. We tested a few recipes with hard red wheat berries. Yes, they worked. But the baked goods were chewier and denser—and worst of all, in some cases drier. They also didn't last very long at room temperature because of the way the harder wheat berries sucked the moisture right out of the dough. So the best success comes from soft white wheat berries. Look for them at large supermarkets, at health food stores, or from online suppliers.

• **Unsweetened cocoa powder.** Whatever you do, do not use instant cocoa mix. Unsweetened cocoa powder comes in two varieties: natural and Dutch-processed, the latter with an added alkali in the mix that darkens the color, mutes the taste a tad, and helps the powder dissolve more easily. Either will work in these recipes.

• **Milk and other dairy products.** In general, we calibrated these recipes for whole milk and whole-milk products like sour cream or yogurt. Because we're grinding our own flour in the machine, we need a little extra oomph to make sure the baked goods are moist and tender. That said, we'll let you know when you can use *low-fat* milk (almost always 2 percent) or other, low-fat dairy products. As a general rule, *fat-free* sour cream or yogurt will not work in these recipes.

• **Butter.** Yes, we'll use a lot for baking. It's best to use *unsalted butter*. After all, why let someone else control the salt content of your desserts? But beyond custards and batters, we also almost always use butter to grease the inside of muffin cups, baking pans, and cake pans. You can indeed skip our step and use nonstick spray. Always use the spray that mimics what the recipe requires: either plain nonstick spray for those that only require greasing or so-called "baker's spray" for those that require greasing and flouring.

STEP 4: GET ONE MORE NECESSARY TOOL.

To complete some of these recipes, we recommend you use a specialty tool you've probably never used in baking: an instant-read meat thermometer or a laser thermometer. You'll need it for many of the custards—that is, many of the ice creams, puddings, panna cottas, cream pies, and ice box cakes. We'll get to the whys and wherefores in later sections. Suffice it to say that since the turbo blender is powerful enough to heat the custard to its set point (most often 170°F, sometimes around 160°F), we need a precise measure of that temperature. We can't "coat the back of a wooden spoon" as we do in many stovetop custard recipes, since we're working inside a super-powerful blender that produces an incredible vortex of ingredients. And we can't really see the precise changes of the custard down inside the canister. We need to take the temperature, so we need either an instant-read thermometer (around $20) or a much fancier laser thermometer (again, around $20). Look for them in cookware stores and from their online outlets. Yes, you can get by without a thermometer. But you may have a few more failures. A word to the wise should be sufficient.

SO LET'S GET TO BAKING! It's fun to be part of a culinary revolution. It's even more fun to eat the results.

PUDDINGS, PANNA COTTAS, & ICE CREAMS

We're off to the recipes for rich chocolate pudding, silky marmalade panna cotta, and smooth, fresh raspberry ice cream from your high-horsepower, high-rpm blender. We won't need another bowl or the stove. We won't need to stir and stir. In fact, we won't need to do much at all to create some of the lightest, creamiest treats around. Does that sound like a miracle? No, it's just science. The blades of these turbo blenders produce so much friction (and therefore so much heat) that we can get eggs to set in puddings, custards, and other creamy desserts.

TWO STEPS TO SUCCESS

1. Add the liquids (usually milk and/or cream) as well as most of the other ingredients to the large canister, then turn the machine to high and wait for the mixture inside to get steamy hot, usually somewhere between 120°F and 130°F, if you're inclined to measure. You don't need to, although it can't hurt. Mostly, you're just looking for steam.

2. Add some sort of thickener—cornstarch, flour, what have you—and let the machine run at high speed until (most important) the mixture's temperature reaches 170°F, or until (much, much less important) it looks something like a very smooth thick milk shake. Now you're ready either to pour it into ramekins to firm up in the fridge or to chill it in the canister to get it ready for an ice cream machine.

TAKING THE TEMPERATURE

Listen, you're not using bowls, dirtying utensils, or turning on the stove. So taking the mixture's temperature is a minor inconvenience, right? As we've already mentioned, invest in a laser thermometer or an instant-read meat thermometer for the best results.

- **For a laser thermometer.** Drop the speed to low (you don't have to turn the machine off) and point the laser into the central swirl—aka the vortex. Measure several places along its walls. Most laser thermometers require you to pull the trigger again to take a subsequent measurement. You're looking for a general consensus of 170°F with maybe a couple of points below that temperature, several points above it, and no more than one point at or near 180°F.

- **For an instant-read meat thermometer.** Make sure the probe is cleaned. Turn the blender off. Insert the probe fairly far down into the custard for an accurate reading.

Always remember to cover the blender again if you will continue blending to get the mixture hotter.

Please note that 170°F is the magic number. Yes, the temperature can be a degree or two above that mark. It shouldn't be below. At a little over 180°F, the eggs will definitely begin to scramble. So don't walk away. It sounds complicated, but you'll get the hang of it in no time.

Some recipes are finished at slightly lower temperatures: 160°F, for instance. These are clearly marked. Don't worry: we're beyond the safety mark for raw eggs at that point. But we use this lower temperature when certain ingredients like chocolate can thicken a custard on their own—and thus, the mixture can get way too thick by the time it crawls all the way up to 170°F. We opt for a slightly lower temperature to save the machine's motor excessive effort.

SO LET'S HEAD OFF to the first recipes for custards. The pies, ice box cakes, and cheesecakes are up in the next chapter. For now, you'll just have to settle for butterscotch pudding. And marmalade panna cotta. And strawberry ice cream. And if that's not enough, you might check out the outrageous Snickers bar ice cream. We have—over and over again.

PUDDINGS

HOW ABOUT PUDDING AS A ONE-CANISTER PROCESS? THE CHOCOLATE DOESN'T NEED TO BE CHOPPED, THE EGGS DON'T NEED TO BE TEMPERED, AND OTHER PIECES OF KITCHEN EQUIPMENT CAN STAY CLEAN ON THE SHELVES. WOW!

What's more, that high-horsepower blender will produce just about the creamiest pudding you've ever had. Because the blender works so efficiently, it will get rid of any lumps or stray bits of cooked egg. And forget about those unfortunate hot spots that can develop in a saucepan on the stovetop and result in a compromised, grainy texture.

As we've written, the basic technique here involves two stages: 1) around 120°F and then 2) at 170°F. It's not crucial that you take the mixture's temperature at the first stage. Just look for steam. As you get the hang of making turbo blender puddings, you'll be able to tell when you reach the first stage simply by putting your hands on the outside of the canister and feeling its warmth. But save such loosey-goosey techniques until you're a pro. The second temperature, the higher one, is more crucial. Follow the recipe here, even if you're a pro.

Also, honor the ingredients. Don't use fat-free milk unless the recipe specifically says you can. And use the stated thickeners: cornstarch or flour, for example. We developed these puddings to set under very specific conditions.

And yes, you'll need to plan a bit. These must spend time in the fridge before you can enjoy them.

ABOUT PUDDING SKIN

Unless you take precautions (or add chemical stabilizers), almost all puddings will develop a thickened layer on top, called the "skin." Some people (like us) love the skin, a little bit of chewy, homespun goodness that reminds us of pudding when we were kids. We just cover the ramekins by sealing the plastic wrap across the top lip. But if that skin bothers you, lay a piece of plastic wrap directly on the pudding's surface after it has cooled in the fridge for 30 minutes or so. This barrier will keep the casein in the milk from interacting with air and so keep that (dreaded?) skin from forming.

THERE'S ONLY ONE thing more to add: you're going to need a bunch of ramekins!

VANILLA PUDDING

Here's the classic, so easy and smooth! And get this: you don't even have to set the eggs out so they'll be room temperature, a common recipe task. The blender will heat them up just fine! We opted for cornstarch as our thickener (rather than flour) because we wanted a silky, clean vanilla pudding, one that wasn't cloudy or chewy. If you want to up your game, omit the vanilla extract; instead, split a vanilla bean in half lengthwise and scrape the tiny black seeds into the canister when you add the salt. • MAKES 4 TO 6 SERVINGS

3 cups whole or 2 percent milk

½ cup granulated white sugar

4 large egg yolks

3 tablespoons cornstarch

1½ tablespoons unsalted butter

2 teaspoons pure vanilla extract

¼ teaspoon salt, optional (see Note)

1. Put the milk, sugar, and egg yolks in the large canister. Cover and blend at the highest speed until steaming (about 120°F), approximately 4 minutes.

2. Add the cornstarch, butter, vanilla, and salt, if using. Cover and blend at the highest speed, venting the lid if necessary, until viscous and the temperature reaches 170°F, about 2 minutes.

3. Divide the pudding evenly among four to six medium ramekins or custard cups. Refrigerate until set, about 6 hours. When cold, cover with plastic wrap and store in the fridge for up to 4 days.

NOTE: The salt is optional because it's culinary dynamite. Some people like a little in their desserts to underline subtler flavors. Others prefer a lighter, less layered set of flavors. And, of course, some people are on salt-restrictive diets.

CHOCOLATE PUDDING

Talk about dense! This chocolate pudding uses only unsweetened chocolate for the most intense flavor. Nothing impedes its sweet, slightly bitter extravagance. Buy the finest chocolate you can comfortably afford. Read the labels to discover chocolate made only with cocoa solids, cocoa butter, sugar, and perhaps lecithin, a common stabilizer. Avoid any with shortening or "natural flavors" in the mix. Want it even richer? Add up to 2 tablespoons unsalted butter with the flour. MAKES 4 TO 6 SERVINGS

2 cups whole or 2 percent milk

⅔ cup granulated white sugar

2 ounces unsweetened chocolate (see Note)

¼ cup all-purpose flour

2 large egg yolks

1 teaspoon pure vanilla extract

¼ teaspoon salt, optional

1. Put the milk, sugar, and chocolate in the large canister. Cover and blend at the highest speed until the chocolate has melted and the mixture is steaming (about 120°F), approximately 4 minutes.

2. Add the flour, egg yolks, vanilla, and salt, if using. Cover and blend at the highest speed, venting the lid if necessary, until slightly thickened into milk-shake texture and the temperature reaches 170°F, about 2 minutes.

3. Divide the pudding evenly among four or six medium ramekins or custard cups. Refrigerate until set, at least 6 hours. When cold, cover with plastic wrap and store in the fridge for up to 4 days.

NOTE: While there's no need to chop the chocolate, you don't want a single big chunk in the blender. We assume you're using those 1-ounce squares. If not, chop the chocolate into similarly sized bits.

BUTTERSCOTCH PUDDING

There's no bottled butterscotch flavoring here. Instead, you'll use the blender to create real butterscotch. Once again, if you want it richer, add up to 2 tablespoons unsalted butter with the flour and cornstarch.

MAKES 4 TO 6 SERVINGS

2 cups whole or 2 percent milk

½ cup heavy cream

⅓ cup packed dark brown sugar

4 large egg yolks

2 teaspoons pure vanilla extract

¼ teaspoon salt

¼ cup all-purpose flour

2½ tablespoons cornstarch

1. Put the milk, cream, brown sugar, egg yolks, vanilla, and salt in the large canister. Cover and blend at the highest speed until steaming (about 120°F), approximately 4 minutes.

2. Add the flour and cornstarch. Cover and blend at the highest speed, venting the lid if necessary, until the mixture reaches 170°F, about 2 minutes.

3. Divide the pudding evenly among four to six medium ramekins or custard cups. Refrigerate until set, at least 6 hours. When cold, cover with plastic wrap and store in the fridge for up to 4 days.

PEANUT BUTTER PUDDING

Peanut butter acts as its own thickener in this pudding. In fact, the machine's motor may drag a bit as the pudding comes together. If the motor strains because the mixture is too thick, stop it and continue to step 3. Once the mixture is at 160°F, the eggs are safe and you're good to go! · MAKES 4 TO 6 SERVINGS

3 cups whole or 2 percent milk

¾ cup granulated white sugar

½ cup peanut butter (of any sort)

I large egg, plus 2 large egg yolks

I tablespoon pure vanilla extract

2 tablespoons cornstarch

1. Put the milk, sugar, peanut butter, egg yolks, and vanilla in the large canister. Cover and blend at the highest speed until steaming (about 120°F), approximately 4 minutes.

2. Add the cornstarch. Cover and blend at the highest speed, venting the lid if necessary, until the mixture reaches 170°F, about 2 minutes.

3. Scrape the pudding out of the canister, dividing it evenly among six medium ramekins or custard cups. Refrigerate until set, at least 6 hours. When cold, cover with plastic wrap and store in the fridge for up to 3 days.

CHAI TEA PUDDING

Chai tea is made from black tea and a blend of warming spices like cinnamon, nutmeg, and cardamom. It turns this pudding into comfort food for a chilly fall day. The mixture will thicken quite a bit in the blender and maybe indeed strain the machine before it reaches 170°F. Stop the motor if you feel too much drag. The pudding will be hot and ready to set. • MAKES 4 SERVINGS

2 cups whole or 2 percent milk

2 tablespoons loose chai tea or 3 small chai tea bags

½ cup sweetened condensed milk

3 large egg yolks

1 tablespoon pure vanilla extract

3 tablespoons cornstarch

1. Pour the milk into a microwave-safe bowl and microwave on high until hot but not boiling, stirring occasionally, about 1 minute. Stir in the chai tea and set aside to steep for 5 minutes.

2. Strain the liquid to remove the spices, or simply remove the tea bags. (Discard the spices or tea bags.) Pour the infused milk into the large canister. Let stand for 5 minutes to cool down just a bit so it doesn't begin to scramble the eggs.

3. Add the sweetened condensed milk, egg yolks, and vanilla. Cover and blend at the highest speed until steaming (about 120°F), approximately 4 minutes.

4. Add the cornstarch. Cover and blend at the highest speed, venting the lid if necessary, until thickened quite a bit and the temperature reaches 170°F, about 2 minutes.

5. Divide the pudding among four medium ramekins or custard cups. Refrigerate until set, about 3 hours. After 6 hours, cover with plastic wrap. Store in the fridge for up to 3 days.

LEMON PUDDING

Lemon juice will begin to thicken this mixture even without much cornstarch. However, let it reach its stated temperature for the creamiest, lightest texture. Use freshly squeezed lemon juice for the best flavor *and* texture.

MAKES 4 TO 6 SERVINGS

1 cup whole or 2 percent milk

1¼ cups sweetened condensed milk (one 14-ounce can)

2 large eggs, plus 2 large egg yolks

¼ cup fresh lemon juice

½ teaspoon lemon extract

2 tablespoons cornstarch

¼ teaspoon salt, optional

1. Put the milk, sweetened condensed milk, eggs, and egg yolks in the large canister. Cover and blend at the highest speed until steaming (about 120°F), approximately 4 minutes.

2. Add the lemon juice, lemon extract, cornstarch, and salt, if using. Cover and blend at the highest speed, venting the lid if necessary, until thickened like a loose lemon curd and the temperature reaches 170°F, about 2 minutes.

3. Divide the pudding evenly among four to six medium ramekins or custard cups. Refrigerate until set, at least 6 hours. When cold, cover with plastic wrap and store in the fridge for up to 4 days.

COCONUT PUDDING

Don't use so-called "lite" or low-fat coconut milk here. You need all the richness of regular coconut milk to help the pudding set. Consider topping each serving with fresh raspberries, sliced strawberries, or even a little chocolate syrup. · MAKES 4 TO 6 SERVINGS

1¾ cups regular coconut milk

1 cup whole or 2 percent milk

½ cup granulated white sugar

½ cup sweetened shredded coconut

6 large egg yolks

3 tablespoons cornstarch

¼ teaspoon salt, optional

1. Put the coconut milk, milk, sugar, shredded coconut, and egg yolks in the large canister. Cover and blend at the highest speed until steaming (about 120°F), approximately 4 minutes.

2. Add the cornstarch and salt, if using. Cover and blend at the highest speed, venting the lid if necessary, until the mixture thickens somewhat but is still pourable, and its temperature reaches 170°F, about 2 minutes.

3. Divide the pudding evenly among four to six medium ramekins or custard cups. Refrigerate until set, at least 6 hours. When cold, cover with plastic wrap and store in the refrigerator for up to 5 days.

PANNA COTTAS

CHOCOLATE PANNA COTTA 20

RASPBERRY PANNA COTTA 20

COFFEE PANNA COTTA 23

MARMALADE PANNA COTTA 23

PANNA COTTA IS A CLASSIC ITALIAN DESSERT, PRIZED FOR ITS LIGHT BUT SLIGHTLY CHEWY TEXTURE. BECAUSE OF THE WAY A TURBO BLENDER WORKS, THESE VERSIONS ARE LESS JIGGLY THAN THE MORE TRADITIONAL PANNA COTTAS.

Those are made by pouring hot cream over gelatin and allowing it to set up in the fridge. These, of course, are simpler.

A NOTE ABOUT INGREDIENTS

We start each recipe by sprinkling unflavored gelatin over a liquid in a small bowl, then setting this mixture aside until the gelatin has "softened"—that is, until the liquid has been completely or mostly absorbed (the recipe will tell you which). Don't shortchange this step.

The gelatin needs to be hydrated to work in the subsequent steps since you'll only mix it into the other ingredients with the blender, rather than heat it up at high speed in the canister.

And, of course, we're talking about unflavored gelatin granules, not Jell-O! Look for the small packets in the baking aisle.

All of these panna cottas involve liqueurs or alcohol, as is traditional in the flavored versions of this dessert. If you want a booze-free offering (the alcohol will not "cook out"), you'll see that you can substitute water in all cases. The flavor will not be as pronounced but you won't have to worry about someone who may not be able to have alcoholic beverages.

SERVING SUGGESTIONS

We like to serve these in stemless wineglasses, but they work in ramekins or custard cups, too. You can even put them in coffee cups or mugs. But you probably can't unmold them. They're a bit more satiny than the standard, since there's more air whipped into each panna cotta.

There may be a bit of separation in some of these as they chill, resulting in a thin layer of clearer liquid underneath the creamier panna cotta. We sort of like these jewel tones, caused by excess moisture in certain brands of jam or preserves or by the gelatin not being thoroughly mixed in. Spoon up the clearer layer with the rest of the panna cotta for the best flavor.

Of course, all of these can be served with a garnish of sweetened whipped cream and a berry or two. You might as well go all out. It's panna cotta, after all.

CHOCOLATE PANNA COTTA

Here's a light, chocolate dessert, best served after a barbecue or a big weekend feast. Bittersweet chocolate, our preference, will give the dessert a slightly more sophisticated finish, probably not a favorite with the elementary school set. Use semisweet chocolate for a milder flavor. In any event, go all out by adding a spoonful of whipped cream to each serving. • MAKES 4 SERVINGS

One ¼-ounce package unflavored gelatin

3 tablespoons crème de cacao, or water

1½ cups whole milk

3 ounces bittersweet or semisweet chocolate

¼ cup granulated white sugar

1 teaspoon pure vanilla extract

⅛ teaspoon salt, optional

¾ cup heavy cream

1. Soak the gelatin in the crème de cacao, or water, in a small bowl until the gelatin has absorbed the liquid, about 5 minutes.

2. Put the milk, chocolate, sugar, vanilla, and salt, if using, in the large canister. Cover and blend at the highest speed until steaming (about 120°F), approximately 4 minutes.

3. Scrape in the gelatin mixture; blend on low speed until dissolved. Add the cream; blend on low speed until smooth.

4. Divide the mixture among four medium ramekins or small wineglasses. Refrigerate for at least 6 hours or until set. Cover with plastic wrap after 8 hours and store in the refrigerator for up to 3 days.

RASPBERRY PANNA COTTA

No amount of blending can cover the taste of inferior raspberry jam. Buy a quality brand for the best success. • MAKES 4 SERVINGS

One ¼-ounce package unflavored gelatin

3 tablespoons raspberry-flavored liqueur (such as Chambord), raspberry-flavored vodka, or water

1½ cups whole milk

¾ cup seedless raspberry jam

¼ cup sugar

⅛ teaspoon salt, optional

⅔ cup heavy cream

1. Soak the gelatin in the liqueur, vodka, or water in a small bowl until the liquid has been absorbed, about 5 minutes.

2. Put the milk, jam, sugar, and salt, if using, in the large canister. Cover and blend at the highest speed until steaming (about 120°F), approximately 4 minutes.

3. Scrape in the gelatin mixture and blend at low speed until dissolved. Add the cream; blend at low speed until smooth.

4. Divide the mixture among four medium ramekins or small wineglasses. Refrigerate for at least 6 hours or until set. Cover with plastic wrap after 8 hours. Store in the refrigerator for up to 3 days.

COFFEE PANNA COTTA

We use a surprise ingredient to keep this dessert super creamy: Marshmallow Fluff (for those east of the Mississippi) or Marshmallow Crème (for the rest of the U. S.). It'll give the panna cotta an incredibly smooth texture, so we also feel free to use low-fat milk. Again, a little sweetened whipped cream on each serving would be a welcome garnish. • MAKES 4 SERVINGS

One ¼-ounce package unflavored gelatin

3 tablespoons coffee-flavored liqueur, espresso, or strong coffee

1½ cups whole or 2 percent milk

¾ cup Marshmallow Fluff or Marshmallow Crème

¼ cup packed dark brown sugar

2 teaspoons instant coffee granules

½ cup heavy cream

1. Soak the gelatin in the liqueur or other liquid in a small bowl until the liquid has been absorbed, about 5 minutes.

2. Put the milk, Marshmallow Fluff or Crème, brown sugar, and instant coffee in the large canister. Cover and blend until steaming (about 120°F), approximately 4 minutes.

3. Scrape in the gelatin mixture and blend on low speed until dissolved. Add the cream and blend on low speed until smooth. Divide the mixture among four medium ramekins or small wineglasses. Refrigerate for at least 6 hours or until set. Cover with plastic wrap after 8 hours. Store in the refrigerator for up to 3 days.

MARMALADE PANNA COTTA

This last panna cotta is perhaps the most unusual in the group. The vanilla will high-light the natural sweet/sour notes in the orange marmalade. This one might be best with a crisp, buttery cookie on the side—or even a graham cracker! • MAKES 6 SERVINGS

One ¼-ounce package unflavored gelatin

3 tablespoons Triple Sec, or orange-flavored liqueur (such as Cointreau), or water

2 cups whole milk

⅔ cup orange marmalade

¼ cup granulated white sugar

2 tablespoons packed light brown sugar

½ teaspoon pure vanilla extract

½ teaspoon orange extract, optional

¾ cup heavy cream

1. Soak the gelatin in the Triple Sec, liqueur, or water in a small bowl until the liquid has been absorbed, about 5 minutes.

2. Put the milk, marmalade, white sugar, brown sugar, vanilla, and orange extract, if using, in the large canister. Cover and blend at the highest speed until steaming, approximately 4 minutes.

3. Scrape in the gelatin mixture and blend at low speed until dissolved, less than a minute. Add the cream and blend at low speed until smooth, less than a minute. Divide the mixture among six medium ramekins or small wineglasses. Refrigerate for at least 6 hours or until set. Cover with plastic wrap after 8 hours. Store in the refrigerator for up to 4 days.

ICE CREAMS

F YOU'RE LOOKING FOR THE *EASIEST* WAY TO MAKE ICE CREAM, YOU NEED TO GET YOUR TURBO BLENDER BUSY. AND IF YOU'RE LOOKING FOR A WAY TO MAKE SOME OF THE *SMOOTHEST* ICE CREAM, YOU STILL NEED TO GET THAT TURBO BLENDER BUSY.

After three cookbooks on ice cream, we may never make it any other way again!

And we're not just talking about plain ol' ice cream. We're talking about frozen custard, rich with eggs and cream. We haven't gone into fancy labeling here; we've called most of these "ice creams" (and a few frozen yogurts). But if there's a heavy pour of cream in the mix and lots of eggs, you can bet you'll get the luxurious, velvety consistency of frozen custard. Move over, Culver's!

A lot of people resort to making ice cream without eggs because they don't want to stir and stir, don't want to temper the eggs, and don't want to fuss with all that cleanup. Well, no more! We can create a custard, then chill the mixture right in the canister until we're ready to freeze it in an ice cream machine.

TWO SMALL PROBLEMS

- **The yields in these ice creams can be tricky.** All these recipes were designed to produce *about* 1 quart. That's the amount you can make in most modern freezer-insert or built-in compressor ice cream machines. You may, however, find you have a tad more custard, based on the exact rpms of your turbo blender. If so, freeze the remainder in a second batch.

- **There's lag time built into these recipes.** These frozen desserts will taste better if you chill the mixture before you freeze it in an ice cream machine. You'll churn less air into the frozen treat and so produce a creamier scoop, more in line with store-bought premium ice cream. Also make sure every part of your ice cream machine is cold: refrigerate (or even freeze) the dasher and the lid for a few hours. The quicker the ice cream freezes, the denser and more luxurious it will be.

THERE'S NO WAY TO CALIBRATE these recipes for every ice cream machine on the market. You'll need to follow the instructions for your model. And remember: ice cream is usually best when it first comes out of the machine, while it's still a little soft. Yes, you can pack it into a container and store it in your freezer for up to 2 weeks, maybe longer. But anyone who has ever come home from the store, taken the lid off the carton, and skimmed the edge knows the truth: the stuff's unbelievable when it's a little melted.

VANILLA ICE CREAM

Let's start off simple: just milk, cream, eggs, sugar, and vanilla. Well, yes, there is flour, too. Most premium frozen custards have some sort of thickener in the mix to protect the eggs. Also, because we're actually adding more air to the custard in the blender, we need to make sure the resulting ice cream is as luxurious as it can be. • MAKES ABOUT 1 QUART

¾ cup whole milk

2 large eggs, plus 2 large egg yolks

¾ cup granulated white sugar

1 tablespoon pure vanilla extract

¼ teaspoon salt, optional

1½ tablespoons all-purpose flour

1½ cups heavy cream

1. Put the milk, eggs, egg yolks, sugar, vanilla, and salt, if using, in the large canister. Cover and blend at the highest speed until steaming (about 120°F), approximately 4 minutes.

2. Add the flour, cover, and blend at the highest speed, venting the lid as necessary, until thickened about like a milk shake and the temperature reaches 170°F, about 2 minutes.

3. Add the cream and blend at low speed until smooth, for just a few seconds. Cover the canister and set it in the refrigerator for at least 6 hours or up to 24 hours.

4. Blend at low speed to recombine. Freeze in an ice cream machine according to your manufacturer's instructions.

NOTE: Add any mix-ins (chocolate chips, nuts, chopped candies, or dried fruit) during the last few churns in the ice cream machine.

HOT FUDGE SAUCE

Good vanilla ice cream needs good chocolate sauce. So does chocolate ice cream. And even butter pecan ice cream. Fortunately, a high-horsepower blender will do the trick without even turning on the stove. This hot fudge sauce is so thick, it'll set up in the fridge. You'll need to microwave small amounts for subsequent sundaes . . . assuming there are subsequent sundaes. • MAKES A HEAVY 3 CUPS

1 cup half-and-half

¼ cup granulated white sugar

¼ cup light corn syrup

8 ounces semisweet chocolate chips or semisweet chocolate, broken into squares or roughly chopped

4 tablespoons (½ stick) unsalted butter

1 teaspoon pure vanilla extract

Up to ½ teaspoon salt

1. Pour the half-and-half, sugar, and light corn syrup in the large canister. Cover and blend at the highest speed until steaming, about 4 minutes.

2. Add the chocolate, butter, vanilla, and salt. Cover and blend at the highest speed until smooth and somewhat thick, 1 to 2 minutes.

3. Pour into a glass or heat-safe plastic container. Cool for 10–15 minutes at room temperature or cover and refrigerate until stiff, at least 4 hours. The sauce can be kept tightly covered in the refrigerator for up to 1 week. To serve, spoon small amounts into a microwave-safe bowl. Microwave on high in 10-second increments, stirring after each, until warm and pourable.

DARK CHOCOLATE ICE CREAM

We're going to take this ice cream mixture to a slightly lower temperature in the canister. For one thing, since the chocolate acts as a thickener, we don't want the mixture to get too sticky. For another, since the eggs are not protected by a thickener, we'll get them to a slightly lower temperature to avoid scrambling them but still stay above the safe temperature. But the results will be a sophisticated chocolate ice cream. • MAKES ABOUT 1 QUART

1 cup whole milk

½ cup granulated white sugar

¼ cup unsweetened cocoa powder

6 ounces bittersweet or semisweet chocolate chips or semisweet chocolate, broken into squares or roughly chopped

2 large egg yolks

1½ cups heavy cream

1 teaspoon pure vanilla extract

1. Put the milk, sugar, cocoa powder, and chocolate in the large canister. Cover and blend at the highest speed until steaming (about 120°F), approximately 4 minutes.

2. Add the egg yolks. Cover and blend at the highest speed, venting the lid if necessary, until smooth and somewhat viscous and the temperature reaches 160°F, 1 to 2 minutes.

3. Add the cream, vanilla, and salt, if using. Blend on low speed until smooth. Cover the canister and refrigerate for at least 6 hours or up to 24 hours.

4. Blend on low speed to recombine. Freeze in an ice cream machine according to the manufacturer's instructions.

CHOCOLATE FROZEN YOGURT

Talk about simple—and intense! This is a *tangy* frozen yogurt, not the pale imitation sometimes sold at our supermarkets. For the best flavor, look for Greek-style yogurt without any chemical thickeners. • MAKES 1 SCANT QUART

1 cup whole milk

1¼ cups granulated white sugar

4 ounces unsweetened chocolate, roughly chopped or broken into squares

2 teaspoons pure vanilla extract

1 cup plain, full-fat Greek yogurt

¾ cup heavy cream

1. Put the milk, sugar, chocolate, and vanilla in the large canister. Cover and blend at the highest speed until the chocolate has melted and the mixture is steaming, about 4 minutes. (see Note)

2. Add the yogurt and cream. Blend at low speed until smooth, just a few seconds. Cover the canister and refrigerate for at least 4 hours, or up to 24 hours.

3. Blend at low speed to recombine. Freeze in an ice cream machine according to the manufacturer's instructions.

NOTE: Here there's no need for reading the temperature. You just want the mixture hot enough to melt and smooth out the chocolate.

CHOCOLATE MALT ICE CREAM

Once again, we're going to take this one to a slightly lower temperature than some other custards in this chapter because we have left out any flour or cornstarch in the presence of two natural thickeners: the chocolate and the malt. They're an all-American combo!

MAKES ABOUT 1 QUART

1⅓ cups whole milk

⅔ cup granulated white sugar

¼ cup malted milk powder

2 ounces unsweetened chocolate, roughly chopped or broken into squares

1 large egg, plus 1 large egg yolk

1 cup heavy cream

2 teaspoons pure vanilla extract

¼ teaspoon salt, optional

1. Put the milk, sugar, malted milk powder, chocolate, egg, and egg yolk in the large canister. Cover and blend at the highest speed, venting the lid as necessary, until the mixture reaches 160°F, 6 to 7 minutes.

2. Add the cream, vanilla, and salt, if using. Blend at low speed until smooth, just a few seconds. Cover the canister and refrigerate for at least 6 hours or up to 24 hours.

3. Blend at low speed to recombine. Freeze in an ice cream machine according to the manufacturer's instructions.

STRAWBERRY ICE CREAM

This one's a Philadelphia-style ice cream—that is, it contains no eggs. We're simply heating the ingredients up to get the sugar properly dissolved. But we do want to watch the temperature so the cornstarch has a chance to thicken the ice cream to a better texture. • MAKES ABOUT 1 QUART

2 cups half-and-half

½ cup granulated white sugar

2 tablespoons cornstarch

1 heaping cup hulled small strawberries

½ cup high-quality strawberry jam

1 teaspoon pure vanilla extract

1. Pour the half-and-half and sugar in the large canister. Cover and blend at the highest speed until steaming, about 4 minutes.

2. Add the cornstarch. Cover and blend at the highest speed until thickened like a smooth milk shake and the temperature reaches 170°F, about 2 minutes.

3. Add the strawberries, jam, and vanilla. Cover and blend at low speed until smooth, until the strawberries are pureed, less than a minute. Cover the canister and refrigerate for at least 6 hours or up to 24 hours.

4. Blend at low speed to recombine. Freeze in an ice cream machine according to the manufacturer's instructions.

STRAWBERRY FROZEN YOGURT

Because of the extra moisture from the fruit, this frozen treat is a little icy. Let it stand on the countertop for about ten minutes if you've stored it in a sealed container in the freezer. And remember the rule for all fruit: if it doesn't smell like anything, it probably won't taste like anything. • MAKES ABOUT 1 QUART

1½ cups whole milk

¾ cup granulated white sugar

10 large strawberries, hulled

1 teaspoon pure vanilla extract

¾ cup full-fat plain Greek yogurt

¾ cup heavy cream

1. Put the milk, sugar, strawberries, and vanilla in the large canister. Cover and blend at the highest speed until steaming, about 4 minutes.

2. Add the yogurt and cream. Cover and blend at low speed until smooth, just a few seconds. Cover the canister and refrigerate for at least 4 hours or up to 24 hours.

3. Blend at low speed to recombine. Freeze in an ice cream machine according to the manufacturer's instructions.

NOTE: For a less complex flavor, omit the vanilla extract. For a slightly more sophisticated flavor, substitute balsamic vinegar for the vanilla. If you do, also add ½ teaspoon salt along with the vinegar.

BUTTER PECAN ICE CREAM

Here's an easy way to make one of America's favorite flavors! Why is the higher temperature indicated here when there's no flour or cornstarch in the mix? Because the ground pecans act as the same kind of protection for the eggs. • MAKES ABOUT 1 QUART

¾ cup chopped pecans

1 tablespoon unsalted butter

1½ cups half-and-half

1 cup packed dark brown sugar

1 large egg, plus 1 large egg yolk

1 teaspoon pure vanilla extract

¾ cup heavy cream

1. Combine the pecans and butter in a large skillet set over medium-low heat. Cook, stirring often, until the pecans turn fragrant, about 2 minutes. Scrape half the mixture in the skillet into the blender's large canister; reserve the remainder off the heat.

2. Add the half-and-half, brown sugar, egg, egg yolk, and vanilla. Cover and blend at the highest speed until the temperature reaches 170°F, 6 to 7 minutes.

3. Add the cream and blend at low speed until smooth, just a few seconds. Cover the canister and refrigerate for at least 4 hours or up to 24 hours.

4. Blend at low speed to recombine. Freeze in an ice cream machine according to the manufacturer's instructions. Near the end of the freezing, when the ice cream has set up, add the reserved pecans and let the machine's dasher churn them into the ice cream until well combined, about 1 minute.

PISTACHIO ICE CREAM

By toasting the pistachios, we can get a more complex flavor into the custard, a better match to all that cream. The almond extract will provide only a small ground note among the flavors, something to bring the natural sweetness of the pistachios forward. You can omit it, of course, for a simpler palette.

MAKES ABOUT 1 QUART

⅔ cup shelled, unsalted pistachios (see Note)

1¼ cups heavy cream

¾ cup whole milk

½ cup granulated white sugar

3 large egg yolks

¼ teaspoon salt

¼ teaspoon almond extract, optional

1. Heat the oven to 350°F with the rack positioned in the center. Spread the pistachios on a large, rimmed baking sheet. Toast in the oven for about 10 minutes, stirring occasionally, until lightly browned and fragrant. Transfer to the large canister of a blender. Cool for 10 minutes.

2. Add the cream, milk, sugar, egg yolks, salt, and almond extract, if using. Cover and blend at the highest speed until the mixture's temperature reaches 170°F, about 2 minutes. Cover the canister and refrigerate for at least 4 hours or up to 24 hours.

3. Blend at low speed to recombine. Freeze in an ice cream machine according to the manufacturer's instructions.

NOTE: Unsalted pistachios can be hard to track down. You can use salted ones but rinse them repeatedly in a strainer set in the sink and dry them well with paper towels. Omit the salt, of course. The resulting ice cream will still be salty as well as softer, not quite as firmly set.

PEANUT BRITTLE ICE CREAM

Now we're just being mad scientists! But since we can grind peanut brittle into ice cream, we might as well. Look for high-quality peanut brittle made with plenty of butter and peanuts. We wouldn't want anything less. • MAKES ABOUT 1 QUART

1¼ cups regular evaporated milk

1 cup purchased, broken-up peanut brittle (about 6 ounces)

¼ cup packed light brown sugar

1½ cups heavy cream

1. Place the evaporated milk, peanut brittle, and brown sugar in the large canister. Cover and blend at the highest speed until steaming, 3 to 4 minutes.

2. Add the cream and blend at low speed until smooth, just a few seconds. Cover the canister and refrigerate for at least 3 hours or up to 24 hours.

3. Blend at low speed to recombine. Freeze in an ice cream machine according to the manufacturer's instructions.

PEACH ICE CREAM

This peach ice cream isn't chunky. We find that peach pieces often become icy bombs in the smooth custard. However, if you miss them, add ½ cup chopped, pitted, fresh peach to the ice cream in the machine during its last few turns. · MAKES ABOUT 1 QUART

1½ cups half-and-half

⅔ cup granulated white sugar

⅓ cup peach nectar

2 large, sweet, ripe peaches, pitted

¾ cup heavy cream

¼ teaspoon pure vanilla extract

¼ teaspoon salt, optional

1. Pour the half-and-half, sugar, and peach nectar into the large canister. Cover and blend at the highest speed until steaming, about 3 minutes. (see Note)

2. Add the peaches, cream, vanilla, and salt, if using. Blend at low speed until smooth, about 1 minute. Cover the canister and refrigerate for at least 3 hours or up to 24 hours.

3. Blend at low speed to recombine. Freeze in an ice cream machine according to the manufacturer's instructions.

NOTE: Since there are no eggs in this ice cream, we don't need to worry about temperature.

RASPBERRY ICE CREAM

If you're opposed to raspberry seeds, buy seedless raspberry jam, then pour the ice cream mixture through a fine-mesh sieve or a colander lined with cheesecloth after step 3 and before you chill it. · MAKES ABOUT 1 QUART

½ cup whole milk

½ cup granulated white sugar

¼ cup raspberry jam

2 tablespoons cornstarch

2 cups raspberries (about 4½ ounces)

1¼ cups heavy cream

⅛ teaspoon salt, optional

1. Put the milk, sugar, and raspberry jam in the large canister. Cover and blend at the highest speed until steamy, about 4 minutes.

2. Add the cornstarch. Cover and blend at the highest speed until fairly thickened and the mixture's temperature reaches 170°F, about 2 minutes.

3. Add the raspberries, cream, and salt, if using. Blend at low speed until smooth, less than 1 minute. Cover the canister and refrigerate for at least 4 hours or up to 24 hours.

4. Blend at low speed to recombine. Freeze in an ice cream machine according to the manufacturer's instructions.

LEMON ICE CREAM

Yes, lemon juice curdles milk. But we don't have to worry about that problem because we're essentially making a loose, light lemon curd in the blender, then just adding cream to it. The resulting ice cream is smooth and incredibly rich, a real treat on a hot summer day. • MAKES ABOUT 1 QUART

1 cup granulated white sugar

½ cup fresh lemon juice

2 large eggs

2 tablespoons unsalted butter

2 cups heavy cream

1 teaspoon lemon extract

⅛ teaspoon salt, optional

1. Put the sugar, lemon juice, eggs, and butter in the large canister. Cover and blend at the highest speed until steaming and the mixture's temperature registers 150°F, about 5 minutes. (See Note)

2. Add the cream, extract, and salt, if using. Blend at low speed until smooth, just a few seconds. Cover the canister and refrigerate for at least 4 hours or up to 24 hours.

3. Blend at low speed to recombine. Freeze in an ice cream machine according to the manufacturer's instructions.

NOTE: Pay attention to the slightly higher temperature that the curd needs to reach to set in step 1.

BANANA ICE CREAM

Because bananas enrich this ice cream, we don't need any eggs or thickeners. That said, we do need ripe bananas. They should have plenty of brown spots and even be a tad soft, probably beyond the point where you'd slice them onto cereal. • MAKES ABOUT 1 QUART

1½ cups half-and-half

⅔ cup granulated white sugar

2 very ripe, medium bananas, peeled

½ cup heavy cream

2 tablespoons banana liqueur, such as crème de banane, or banana syrup, optional

¼ teaspoon salt, optional

1. Put the half-and-half and sugar in the large canister. Cover and blend at the highest speed until steaming, about 4 minutes.

2. Add the bananas, cream, banana liqueur, if using, and salt, if using. Blend at low speed until smooth, about 20 seconds. Cover the canister and refrigerate for at least 3 hours or up to 24 hours.

3. Blend at low speed to recombine. Freeze in an ice cream machine according to the manufacturer's instructions.

PINEAPPLE ICE CREAM

Fresh pineapple has an enzyme that will curdle milk. But by using pineapple jam, we can create a refreshing, tropical treat without any worries. If you want a more sophisticated flavor, add up to ½ teaspoon rum extract in place of the vanilla extract. • MAKES ABOUT 1 QUART

1 cup pineapple jam

1 cup Marshmallow Fluff or Marshmallow Crème

1½ cups heavy cream

½ cup whole milk

1 teaspoon pure vanilla extract

1. Combine all the ingredients in the large canister. Cover and blend at the highest speed until smooth, about 30 seconds. (see Note)

2. Freeze in an ice cream machine according to the manufacturer's instructions.

NOTE: We don't really need to heat this mixture, just get it smooth. Thus, we can freeze it in the machine just after making it. Of course, you can also always store the covered canister in your fridge for several hours.

CHOCOLATE CREAM COOKIES AND CREAM ICE CREAM

No, we're not talking cookies folded into ice cream. We're using a turbo blender! We're talking about grinding the cookies right into the mixture for the most intense flavor imaginable. You're welcome. • MAKES ABOUT 1 QUART

2 cups heavy cream

1 cup whole milk

⅔ cup granulated white sugar

1 teaspoon pure vanilla extract

12 Oreo, Hydrox, or other chocolate sandwich cream cookies

1. Put the cream, milk, sugar, and vanilla in the large canister. Cover and blend at the highest speed until steaming, about 4 minutes. (See Note) Refrigerate the mixture in the covered canister until cold, for at least 3 hours or up to 24 hours.

2. Add the cookies and pulse to combine, until they're crushed through the mixture. Freeze in an ice cream machine according to the manufacturer's instructions.

NOTE: Why do we worry about bringing this to a steaming temperature if there are no eggs in the mix? Because warming the cream helps the sugar dissolve more evenly and gives the overall ice cream a better texture.

PEANUT BUTTER COOKIES AND CREAM ICE CREAM

You might want to save a few cookies to serve on the side. Or not. Because the ice cream itself will taste just like the cookies anyway—only colder, richer, and more enticing. • MAKES ABOUT 1 QUART

2 cups half-and-half

¾ cup granulated white sugar

2 large eggs

½ cup heavy cream

½ cup creamy peanut butter

8 peanut butter sandwich cookies (such as Nutter Butter Peanut Butter Sandwich Cookies)

1. Put the half-and-half, sugar, and eggs in the large canister. Cover and blend at the highest speed until the mixture's temperature reaches 170°F, about 6 minutes.

2. Add the cream and peanut butter. Blend at low speed until smooth, about 20 seconds. Cover the canister and refrigerate for at least 4 hours or up to 24 hours.

3. Add the cookies and pulse just until they're coarsely ground and even throughout the cream mixture. Freeze in an ice cream machine according to the manufacturer's instructions.

NOTE: The texture in step 3 is a matter of taste. You can leave the cookies in small chunks, about the size of chocolate chips. Or you can pulse further, giving the ice cream a grainier texture but more intense cookie flavor.

MINT CHOCOLATE CHIP ICE CREAM

Here's the miracle of a turbo blender in action. We actually grind the peppermint patties into the custard to add richness and body. It's smooth and luscious, with a far more intense flavor than standard offerings. It'll also cool you down on a hot summer day! MAKES ABOUT 1 QUART

1½ cups half-and-half

¾ cup broken-up chocolate-covered Peppermint Patties

¼ cup granulated white sugar

1 cup heavy cream

½ cup mini chocolate chips

1. Put the half-and-half, Peppermint Patties, and sugar in the large canister. Cover and blend at the highest speed until smooth and steaming, about 4 minutes.

2. Add the cream and blend at low speed until smooth, just a few seconds. Cover the canister and refrigerate for at least 3 hours or up to 24 hours.

3. Blend at low speed to recombine. Freeze in an ice cream machine according to the manufacturer's instructions. When the ice cream has set, add the chips and let the machine's dasher stir them into the ice cream until evenly distributed, about 1 minute.

NOTE: The ice cream will not be green, as traditional mint ice cream often is. If desired, add up to 2 or 3 drops of green food coloring with the heavy cream.

ALMOND ICE CREAM

Here's an ice cream we couldn't make without a turbo blender: we grind almond paste into a thick, custard-like mixture, then add some cream and chill it down. The results are decadent! But you can still take it over the top with some Hot Fudge Sauce (page 27).
MAKES ABOUT 1 QUART

1 cup whole milk

5 ounces almond paste (see Note)

½ cup granulated white sugar

2 large eggs

1 cup heavy cream

½ teaspoon almond extract

¼ teaspoon salt, optional

1. Put the milk, almond paste, sugar, and eggs in the large canister. Cover and blend at the highest speed until fairly thickened and the temperature reaches 170°F, 6 to 7 minutes.

2. Add the cream, almond extract, and salt, if using. Blend at low speed until smooth, just a few seconds. Cover the canister and refrigerate for at least 4 hours or up to 24 hours.

3. Blend at low speed to recombine. Freeze in an ice cream machine according to the manufacturer's instructions.

NOTE: Almond paste is a mixture of ground almonds and sugar. It's sometimes sold as "marzipan"—but don't buy colored marzipan candies for this recipe. Look for tubes or cans of almond paste in the baking aisle.

SALT CARAMEL ICE CREAM

The mix of salt and caramel is almost irresistible. If you're hesitant about the amount of salt, use only ¼ teaspoon the first time around. With the full amount of salt, the ice cream will never completely firm up, even after it's sat in a container in your freezer for a while. • **MAKES ABOUT 1 QUART**

1½ cups whole milk

3 large egg yolks

¼ cup granulated white sugar

¾ cup heavy cream

¾ cup purchased caramel sauce or ice cream topping

Up to ½ teaspoon salt

1. Put the milk, egg yolks, and sugar in the large canister. Cover and blend at the highest speed until the mixture's temperature reaches 170°F, about 6 minutes.

2. Add the cream, caramel sauce or topping, and salt. Blend at low speed until smooth, just a few seconds. Cover the canister and refrigerate for at least 4 hours or up to 24 hours.

3. Blend at low speed to recombine. Freeze in an ice cream machine according to the manufacturer's instructions.

SNICKERS BAR ICE CREAM

Yep, we're grinding Snickers bars right into the ice cream mixture, turning the whole thing into an incredible treat. We do save some to add in at the end—because we like a few chunks in ours. If you want a fully smooth ice cream, just drop all five candy bars into the blender in step 1.

MAKES ABOUT 1 QUART

1½ cups whole milk

⅓ cup packed dark brown sugar

Five 1.86-ounce Snickers bars

1½ cups heavy cream

1. Put the milk, brown sugar, and 3 of the candy bars in the large canister. Cover and blend at the highest speed until steaming, about 4 minutes. (see Note)

2. Add the cream and blend at low speed until smooth, about 10 seconds. Cover the canister and refrigerate for at least 3 hours or up to 24 hours.

3. Blend at low speed to recombine. Freeze in an ice cream machine according to the manufacturer's instructions. As the ice cream freezes, chop the remaining 2 candy bars into small bits. When the ice cream has set, add the chopped candy bars and let the machine's dasher churn them into the ice cream until evenly distributed, about 1 minute.

NOTE: Make sure the chocolate has a chance to melt in step 1 to get a uniform consistency for a smooth ice cream.

BUTTERFINGER ICE CREAM

Here's why you got that turbo blender: so you can make a creamy ice cream that tastes just like one of North America's favorite candy bars. See: money well spent.

MAKES ABOUT 1 QUART

Four 2.1-ounce Butterfinger candy bars

1¼ cups whole milk

¼ cup granulated white sugar

1½ cups heavy cream

1. Put the candy bars, milk, and sugar in the large canister. Cover and blend at the highest speed until steaming, about 4 minutes.

2. Add the cream. Blend at low speed until smooth, just a few seconds. Cover the canister and refrigerate for at least 3 hours or up to 24 hours.

3. Blend at low speed to recombine. Freeze in an ice cream machine according to the manufacturer's instructions.

MOUNDS BAR ICE CREAM

Here's a terrific combination of coconut and chocolate, just like the candy bar itself. The ice cream tastes best when it's not rock hard out of the freezer but rather when it's fresh out of the machine. If you have saved it in a container in the freezer, let it sit out on the countertop for 10 minutes or so to get good and creamy. • MAKES ABOUT 1 QUART

1 cup regular coconut milk

Four 1.75-ounce packages Mounds candy bars (8 small bars)

½ cup packed light brown sugar

1½ cups heavy cream

1. Put the coconut milk, candy bars, and brown sugar in the large canister. Cover and blend at the highest speed until steaming, about 4 minutes.

2. Add the cream and blend at low speed until smooth, just a few seconds. Cover the canister and refrigerate for at least 3 hours or up to 24 hours.

3. Blend at low speed to recombine. Freeze in an ice cream machine according to the manufacturer's instructions.

CRACKER JACK ICE CREAM

What a surprising treat! The ice cream will taste best either when it's right out of the machine or when it's been allowed to sit at room temperature from the freezer for a few minutes. The popcorn flavor is pretty subtle, so the mix needs to rise a few degrees in temperature to really come through.

MAKES ABOUT 1 QUART

4 cups Cracker Jack popcorn and peanuts (omit the prize!)

1¼ cups whole milk

⅓ cup packed light brown sugar

1½ cups heavy cream

1. Put the Cracker Jacks, milk, and brown sugar in the large canister. Cover and blend at the highest speed until steaming, about 4 minutes.

2. Add the cream. Blend at low speed until smooth, about 10 seconds. Cover the canister and refrigerate for at least 3 hours or up to 24 hours.

3. Blend at low speed to recombine. Freeze in an ice cream machine according to the manufacturer's instructions.

CREAM PIES, ICEBOX CAKES, & CHEESECAKES

IF WE CAN MAKE CUSTARDS AND ICE CREAMS IN A TURBO BLENDER, WE CAN ALSO MAKE LUSCIOUS CREAM PIES, OLD-FASHIONED ICEBOX CAKES, AND ABOUT THE SMOOTHEST CHEESECAKES YOU CAN IMAGINE. NO, THEY'RE NOT CHEWY NEW YORK-STYLE CHEESECAKES. INSTEAD, THEY'RE LIGHTER AND MORE REFRESHING, BETTER ANY TIME OF YEAR. WHAT'S MORE, WE CAN COMPLETE THESE RECIPES IN THE BLENDER CANISTER WITHOUT DIRTYING ANOTHER BOWL OR SAUCEPAN (PROVIDED YOU BUY A CRUST AT THE STORE). GIVEN HOW EASY AND DELICIOUS THE TURBO BLENDER MAKES A CREAM PIE FILLING, IT'S HARD TO IMAGINE WHY YOU'D MAKE ONE ANY OTHER WAY.

A FEW WORDS ABOUT PATIENCE

You've got to let the custard set up in the refrigerator for several hours. The icebox cakes will require a full day in the fridge. So consider these desserts make-aheads, easing your schedule if you're cooking for a holiday, a celebration, or just a casual get-together.

As with the puddings and ice creams, you'll need a thermometer for a successful outcome. While the custards will have a certain thickened appearance once they're at their set point, make sure you take their temperatures. The visual cues here are often less clear than those for pudding and ice cream. For more information on exactly how you take the temperature of the custard, see page 8.

We end the chapter with five homemade crusts and encourage you to try them out. They'll make any dessert more astounding. But we'll confess up front that after we tested these pies the first time around, we made countless retests using purchased crusts. Boy, they sure made life easier.

A FEW WORDS ABOUT CHOCOLATE

Make sure you pay attention to the differences among unsweetened chocolate (usually about 99% cocoa solids), semisweet (about 50%), and bittersweet (about 65%, a more sophisticated flavor). Use what the recipe requires.

While you don't need to chop the chocolate, it shouldn't hit the canister as one large chunk. If possible, break it into squares. If you're working with a baker's block of chocolate, you must break or chip off bits to measure them anyway. These should be about 2-inch chunks, the right size for the blender.

Of course, you can always use semisweet chocolate chips for the chopped semisweet chocolate. (Some high-end grocery stores even carry bittersweet chocolate chips.) However, there is a vast difference among chocolate chips; some of them are made with artificial flavors and cut with lots of vegetable shortening. Read the labels carefully and buy high-quality chips whenever possible.

SO LET'S GET CRACKING. You probably had no idea a vanilla cream pie or a silky smooth cheesecake was so easy—until now.

CREAM PIES

I S THERE ANYTHING BETTER THAN A CREAM PIE? OR ANYTHING THAT TAKES MORE WORK? WELL, NO MORE! A TURBO BLENDER MAKES A CREAM PIE A SNAP. YOU DON'T EVEN NEED TO TEMPER THE EGGS.

In fact, for almost all of these pies, you don't have to bring those eggs to room temperature before you use them. Just crack them open right out of the refrigerator. The blender will heat them up. Plus, you can make the filling in one canister, then whip some heavy cream in that same turbo blender canister to top the chilled pie later on. Why aren't you making a cream pie right now?

THE SET POINT

As with the puddings and ice creams in the last chapter, the fillings come to their set point by the furious friction of those blades. As the ingredients are whirred in the canister, you'll notice a distinct change in their consistency when the custard starts to thicken. No, it won't be like pudding. You should take its temperature to guarantee success. And then the whole thing still has to set up in the refrigerator. But there are three distinct visual cues:

• The filling mixture will begin to look like melted premium ice cream that still has its smooth texture and body.

• It will have almost no foam on its surface.

• And it will have a satin sheen, almost shiny.

THE PROBLEM WITH CRUSTS

All of these pies were developed for a *homemade* 9-inch crust. However, they can be made in the standard, 6-ounce crust, sold in an aluminum pie plate and available at all North American supermarkets.

But there is one niggle. Those 6-ounce crusts, although labeled as 9 inches in diameter, may be a tad shy in their dimensions. And they are certainly not as deep as a homemade crust in a 9-inch pie plate. So there may be a little extra custard left over in the canister once you've filled the shell. If so, pour it into custard cups and refrigerate until set, enjoying it as an afternoon or evening treat in the days ahead. What could be better? Oh, right: a cream pie in minutes without a sink full of bowls and pans.

VANILLA CREAM PIE WITH TURBO BLENDER WHIPPED CREAM

We'll start with the most basic cream pie: rich without being overwhelming. Take it over the top, omit the vanilla and substitute the tiny seeds scraped from a vanilla bean pod. Although we recommend a cookie crust, feel free to substitute a graham cracker crust.

MAKES ONE 9-INCH PIE

1¼ cups whole milk

1 cup sweetened condensed milk

2 large eggs

1 tablespoon pure vanilla extract

¼ teaspoon salt, optional

3 tablespoons cornstarch

One 6-ounce purchased vanilla cookie pie crust or one 9-inch homemade Vanilla Cookie Crust (page 84)

Turbo Blender Whipped Cream (recipe follows)

1. Place the milk, sweetened condensed milk, eggs, vanilla, and salt, if using, in the large canister. Cover and blend at the highest speed until steaming (about 120°F), approximately 4 minutes.

2. Add the cornstarch. Cover and blend at the highest speed, venting the lid if necessary, until fairly well thickened, about like melted premium ice cream, and the temperature reaches 170°F, about 2 minutes.

3. Pour the filling into the prepared crust; refrigerate until cold and set, at least 6 hours or up to 24 hours, covering with plastic wrap once cool. Mound, pipe, or dollop Turbo Blender Whipped Cream over the cold pie.

TURBO BLENDER WHIPPED CREAM

You'll never make whipped cream any other way! The high-horsepower blender makes it dense and creamy. Watch carefully: pulse the machine a few times once the cream starts to thicken. We like whipped cream slightly loose, more like a sauce. You might like it stiffer. But remember there's a fine line between whipped cream and butter. • MAKES ABOUT 3½ CUPS WHIPPED CREAM

3 cups heavy cream

¼ cup confectioners' sugar

2 teaspoons pure vanilla extract, optional

1. Put the cream, confectioners' sugar, and vanilla, if using, in a cleaned and dried large canister. Cover and blend at the highest speed, stopping the machine and scraping down the inside of the canister once, until the mixture is thickened whipped cream, 15 to 20 seconds.

CHOCOLATE CREAM PIE

Skip those instant fillings loaded with chemicals. Make this childhood favorite if only because it's so easy, so real, *and* so intensely chocolaty. For a denser pie, omit the butter and add an additional ½ ounce unsweetened chocolate and 1 tablespoon granulated white sugar. If desired, add an additional 2 tablespoons confectioners' sugar to the Turbo Blender Whipped Cream for a sweeter topping that's a better contrast to the chocolate filling. • MAKES ONE 9-INCH PIE

2 cups whole milk

½ cup granulated white sugar

3 large egg yolks

3½ ounces semisweet chocolate chips or semisweet chocolate, broken into squares or roughly chopped

1½ ounces unsweetened chocolate, broken into squares or roughly chopped

1 tablespoon unsalted butter

½ teaspoon pure vanilla extract

¼ teaspoon salt, optional

¼ cup cornstarch

One 6-ounce purchased chocolate cookie pie crust or one 9-inch homemade Chocolate Sandwich Cookie Crust (page 84)

Turbo Blender Whipped Cream (page 52) or purchased whipped cream

1. Put the milk, sugar, egg yolks, both kinds of chocolate, the butter, vanilla, and salt, if using, in the large canister. Cover and blend at the highest speed until the chocolate melts and the mixture is steaming (about 120°F), approximately 4 minutes.

2. Add the cornstarch. Cover and blend at the highest speed, venting the lid if necessary, until fairly well thickened, about like melted premium chocolate ice cream, and the temperature reaches 170°F, about 2 minutes.

3. Pour the filling into the crust. Refrigerate until set and cold, at least 6 hours or up to 24 hours, covering with plastic wrap once chilled. Mound, pipe, or spread whipped cream over the cold pie just before serving.

NOTE: For a deeper chocolate flavor, substitute bittersweet chocolate for the semisweet.

BANANA CREAM PIE

Look for bananas that are a little riper than perfect for eating on their own. They need to be soft to have enough flavor to stand up to the custard. If you prefer an even more decadent pie, drizzle chocolate syrup over the chilled filling before topping it with whipped cream. • MAKES ONE 9-INCH PIE

One 6-ounce purchased vanilla cookie pie crust or one 9-inch homemade Vanilla Cookie Crust (page 84)

2 small, very ripe bananas, peeled and thinly sliced

2 cups whole milk

⅓ cup granulated white sugar

2 large egg yolks

1 teaspoon pure vanilla extract

1 teaspoon banana extract, optional

6 tablespoons cornstarch

Turbo Blender Whipped Cream (page 52) or purchased whipped cream

1. Lay the banana slices in the prepared crust.

2. Put the milk, sugar, egg yolks, vanilla extract, and banana extract, if using, in the large canister. Cover and blend at the highest speed until steaming (about 120°F), approximately 4 minutes.

3. Add the cornstarch. Cover and blend at the highest speed, venting the lid if necessary, until fairly well thickened and the temperature reaches 170°F, about 2 minutes.

4. Pour and spread the filling into the prepared crust, taking care not to dislodge the bananas. Refrigerate until cold and set, at least 6 hours or up to 24 hours. Mound, pipe, or spread whipped cream over the cold pie.

RASPBERRY CREAM PIE

Because we're adding raspberries late in the blending process for this super smooth filling, make sure those berries are at room temperature. Cold, they'll chill the custard and stop it from setting. Don't use frozen raspberries, even thawed to room temperature. They're too soupy to make a good custard. • MAKES ONE 9-INCH PIE

1¼ cups whole milk

¼ cup heavy cream

⅓ cup granulated white sugar

¼ cup raspberry jam

3 large egg yolks

½ teaspoon pure vanilla extract

1½ cups fresh raspberries (a little less than 7 ounces), at room temperature

6 tablespoons cornstarch

One 6-ounce purchased vanilla cookie pie crust or one 9-inch homemade Vanilla Cookie Crust (page 84)

Turbo Blender Whipped Cream (page 52) or purchased whipped cream

1. Put the milk, cream, sugar, jam, egg yolks, and vanilla in the large canister. Cover and blend at the highest speed until steaming (about 120°F), approximately 4 minutes.

2. Add the raspberries and cornstarch. Cover and blend at the highest speed, venting the lid if necessary, until fairly well thickened and the temperature reaches 170°F, about 2 minutes.

3. Pour the filling into the prepared pie crust. Refrigerate until cold and set, at least 8 hours or up to 48 hours, covering with plastic wrap once chilled. Mound, pipe, or spread whipped cream over the cold pie just before serving.

PUMPKIN PIE

Thanksgiving just got easier! Don't use canned pumpkin pie filling here. You want solid pack pumpkin without other additives. If desired, omit the whipped cream and spread jarred pineapple ice cream topping over the pie before serving. You can still top the pie with whipped cream after that . . . because why not? • MAKES ONE 9-INCH PIE

1½ cups evaporated whole milk

1 cup canned solid-pack 100 percent pumpkin puree

⅔ cup granulated white sugar

1 large egg, plus 1 large egg yolk

¼ teaspoon salt, optional

3 tablespoons cornstarch

One 6-ounce purchased graham cracker pie crust or one 9-inch homemade Graham Cracker Crust (page 84)

Turbo Blender Whipped Cream (page 52) or purchased whipped cream

1. Put the evaporated milk, pumpkin puree, sugar, egg, egg yolk, and salt, if using, in the large canister. Cover and blend at the highest speed until steaming (about 120°F), approximately 4 minutes.

2. Add the cornstarch. Cover and blend at the highest speed, venting the lid if necessary, until the mixture is quite thick and the temperature reaches 160°F, 1 to 2 minutes.

3. Scrape and spread the filling into the prepared crust. Refrigerate until cold and set, at least 6 hours or up to 48 hours, covering with plastic wrap once chilled. Mound, pipe, or spread whipped cream over the cold pie just before serving.

COCONUT CUSTARD PIE

This coconut custard pie uses coconut milk as well as toasted coconut for a double hit of flavor. If you find multiple brands of coconut milk on the grocery store's shelf, shake them lightly to choose the one with the least amount of jostling liquid inside. You'll get more coconut cream in the can and end up with a better pie. We don't call for whipped cream here because the filling is quite rich.

MAKES ONE 9-INCH PIE

2 cups regular coconut milk (see Note)

2 large eggs, plus 2 large egg yolks

⅔ cup granulated white sugar

2 teaspoons pure vanilla extract

¼ teaspoon salt, optional

¼ cup cornstarch

One 6-ounce purchased graham cracker pie crust or one 9-inch homemade Graham Cracker Crust (page 84)

½ cup sweetened shredded coconut

1. Put the coconut milk, eggs, egg yolks, sugar, vanilla, and salt, if using, in the large canister. Cover and blend at the highest speed until steaming (about 120°F), approximately 4 minutes.

2. Add the cornstarch. Cover and blend at the highest speed, venting the lid if necessary, until fairly thickened and the temperature reaches 170°F, about 2 minutes.

3. Pour the filling into the prepared crust. Refrigerate until cold and set, at least 6 hours or up to 24 hours, covering with plastic wrap once chilled.

4. Heat the oven to 300°F with the rack in the center. Spread the coconut on a large, rimmed baking sheet. Toast until lightly browned, stirring occasionally, about 10 minutes. Cool to room temperature, about 1 hour or up to 8 hours. Spread on top of the pie just before serving.

NOTE: Do not substitute cream of coconut, a very sweet mixture, made mostly for tiki drinks.

LEMON BUTTERMILK PIE

Here's an old-fashioned combo with a flavor sort of like chess pie. The filling will be loose, even wet, when you pour it into the pie shell. So long as you've got it at the right temperature, it will indeed set. Fresh lemon juice is also important to its success. If you use bottled, it may be pasteurized and not have enough acid oomph to set the custard.

MAKES ONE 9-INCH PIE

1 cup regular buttermilk

⅔ cup heavy cream

½ cup fresh lemon juice

½ cup granulated white sugar

1 large egg, plus 2 large egg yolks

¼ teaspoon lemon extract

¼ teaspoon salt, optional

3 tablespoons cornstarch

One 6-ounce purchased vanilla cookie pie crust or one 9-inch homemade Vanilla Cookie Crust (page 84)

1. Put the buttermilk, cream, lemon juice, sugar, egg, egg yolks, lemon extract, and salt, if using, in the large canister. Cover and blend at the highest speed until steaming (about 120°F), approximately 4 minutes.

2. Add the cornstarch. Cover and blend at the highest speed, venting the lid if necessary, until somewhat thickened and the temperature reaches 170°F, about 2 minutes.

3. Pour and spread the filling into the prepared crust. Refrigerate until cold and set, at least 8 hours or up to 48 hours, covering with plastic wrap once chilled.

NOTE: If desired, whisk a teaspoon or two of water into raspberry jam until spreadable, then spread over the top of the pie.

KEY LIME PIE

We've added both sweetened condensed milk and coconut to this filling. But if you're going to the trouble of making a key lime pie, why go halfway? We like the extra body the coconut gives to the mixture. Don't worry. It'll be smooth and creamy. The blender will see to that. • MAKES ONE 9-INCH PIE

One 14-ounce can sweetened condensed milk

½ cup fresh or bottled key lime juice

½ cup sweetened shredded coconut

½ cup heavy cream

2 large eggs, plus 2 large egg yolks

¼ teaspoon salt, optional

2 tablespoons cornstarch

One 6-ounce purchased graham cracker pie crust or one 9-inch homemade Graham Cracker Crust (page 84)

Turbo Blender Whipped Cream (page 52) or purchased whipped cream

1. Put the sweetened condensed milk, lime juice, coconut, cream, eggs, egg yolks, and salt, if using, in the large canister. Cover and blend at the highest speed until steaming (about 120°F), approximately 4 minutes.

2. Add the cornstarch. Cover and blend at the highest speed, venting the lid if necessary, until very thick, about like lime curd, and the temperature reaches 160°F, about 1 minute.

3. Spread and smooth the filling into the prepared crust. Refrigerate until cold and set, at least 4 hours or up to 48 hours, covering with plastic wrap once chilled. Mound, pipe, or spread whipped cream over the cold pie just before serving.

GRASSHOPPER PIE

Here's a classic boozy pie, made with two kinds of liqueur for a good kick. It's also made with gelatin for a super-smooth, silky set. If you want, reverse the whipped cream and chocolate: spread whipped cream over the pie, then drizzle each slice with hot fudge sauce.

MAKES ONE 9-INCH PIE

One ¼-ounce packet unflavored gelatin (see Note)

2 tablespoons water

3 large eggs

½ cup granulated white sugar

6 tablespoons whole milk

¼ cup green crème de menthe

¼ cup white (that is, clear) crème de cacao

¼ teaspoon salt, optional

1½ cups heavy cream

Turbo Blender Whipped Cream (page 52) or purchased whipped cream

One 6-ounce purchased chocolate cookie pie crust or one 9-inch homemade Chocolate Sandwich Cookie Crust (page 84)

2 tablespoons purchased hot fudge sauce or homemade Hot Fudge Sauce (page 27)

1. Sprinkle the gelatin over the water in a small bowl. Set aside until all the liquid has been absorbed, about 5 minutes.

2. Put the eggs, sugar, milk, crème de menthe, crème de cacao, and salt, if using, in the large canister. Cover and blend at the highest speed until steaming (about 120°F), approximately 4 minutes.

3. Add the gelatin mixture. Cover and blend at the highest speed, venting the lid if necessary, until well thickened and the temperature reaches 160°F, 1 to 2 minutes. Scrape the mixture into a bowl and cool at room temperature for 30 minutes.

4. Meanwhile, clean and dry the canister. Add the heavy cream, cover, and blend at the highest speed until the mixture is thickened whipped cream, about 10 seconds.

5. Fold the whipped cream into the green mixture until uniform. Spread and smooth the filling into the prepared crust. Refrigerate until cold and set, at least 6 hours or up to 24 hours.

6. Just before serving, soften the hot fudge sauce in a small bowl in the microwave on high for 15 seconds, stirring after every 5 seconds. Cool for 15 minutes at room temperature, stirring occasionally. Drizzle the hot fudge sauce over the pie; top with whipped cream.

NOTE: Of course, we're talking about packets of unflavored granulated gelatin, most often found in the baking aisle—not Jell-O!

SWEET POTATO PIE

We prefer this Southern favorite at Thanksgiving to Pumpkin Pie (page 55) because it offers us a cross between dessert and that classic, holiday side dish! You don't want to grind the mini marshmallows into the custard; rather, chop them just enough to get some in every forkful! · MAKES ONE 9-INCH PIE

One 15-ounce can yams in heavy syrup (do not drain)

1 cup half-and-half

2 large eggs, plus 1 large egg yolk

1 teaspoon pure vanilla extract

¼ teaspoon ground cinnamon

¼ teaspoon freshly grated nutmeg

¼ cup cornstarch

½ cup mini marshmallows

One 6-ounce purchased graham cracker pie crust or one 9-inch homemade Graham Cracker Crust (page 84)

1. Put the yams and their syrup, the half-and-half, eggs, egg yolk, vanilla, cinnamon, and nutmeg in the large canister. Cover and blend at the highest speed until steaming (about 120°F), approximately 4 minutes.

2. Add the cornstarch. Cover and blend at the highest speed, venting the lid if necessary, until considerably thickened and the temperature reaches 160°F, 1 to 2 minutes. Add the mini marshmallows and pulse once to blend in.

3. Pour and scrape the filling into the prepared pie crust. Refrigerate until set and cold, at least 8 hours or up to 48 hours, covering with plastic wrap once chilled.

S'MORES PIE

We turned the campground treat into a pie! But what could be better? The marshmallows will provide a great deal of the body here. But keep your eye on the pie as it browns in the final step—the marshmallows can burn. MAKES ONE 9-INCH PIE

12 ounces semisweet chocolate chips or semisweet chocolate, broken into squares or roughly chopped

1½ cups heavy cream

½ cup whole milk

3 cups mini marshmallows

One 6-ounce purchased graham cracker pie crust or one 9-inch homemade Graham Cracker Crust (page 84)

1. Put the chocolate, cream, and milk in the large canister. Cover and blend at the highest speed until very smooth, like melted hot fudge sauce, 2 to 3 minutes.

2. Add 2 cups of the marshmallows; cover and blend at low speed just until combined and fairly well pureed, with bits of marshmallow here and there, less than 1 minute.

3. Pour and scrape the mixture into the prepared crust. Refrigerate until cold and set, at least 6 hours or up to 48 hours, covering with plastic wrap once chilled.

4. Position an oven rack 10 inches from the broiler; heat the broiler. Spread the remaining 1 cup mini marshmallows over the top of the pie. Set the pie on a large, rimmed baking sheet. Broil until the marshmallows brown a bit and just begin to melt, less than 1 minute. Set in the fridge until cool, about 1 hour, before serving.

CHOCOLATE–CREAM CHEESE PIE

Here's a real treat: a cream cheese pie. Since we're using gelatin as a thickener, we don't have to take the filling mixture to a certain temperature. Besides, we'd risk breaking the cream cheese. But we do need to work with the canister to get this thick mixture to blend properly as it comes together, either by stopping the machine repeatedly to reposition the contents or by using the tamper to keep the mixture constantly on the blades. In fact, we actually add the heavy cream late in the process to keep the mixture from becoming too thick. And that cream needs to be at room temperature so the mixture doesn't break as it blends. The filling is designed for a deeper, homemade crust in a pie plate. If you're using a purchased crust, pour extra filling into ramekins and let them set up in the fridge for an afternoon "pudding" treat.

MAKES ONE 9-INCH PIE

1½ teaspoons unflavored powdered gelatin

1 tablespoon water

1 cup granulated white sugar

8 ounces regular cream cheese

½ cup whole milk

½ cup unsweetened cocoa powder

1 tablespoon pure vanilla extract

¾ cup heavy cream, at room temperature

One 6-ounce purchased chocolate cookie pie crust or one 9-inch homemade Chocolate Sandwich Cookie Crust (page 84)

1. Sprinkle the gelatin over the water in a small microwave-safe bowl or cup. Set aside until all the water has been absorbed, about 5 minutes.

2. Meanwhile, put the sugar, cream cheese, milk, cocoa powder, and vanilla in the large canister. Cover and blend at the highest speed, turning the machine on and off repeatedly so you can scrape down the inside of the canister, or using the tamper, if available, until very smooth and thick, about 1 minute.

3. Microwave the gelatin mixture on high until melted, about 10 seconds. Pour into the canister. Cover and blend at the highest speed until smooth, about 30 seconds.

4. Remove the center knob from the lid. With the blender running at low speed, pour in the cream in a slow drizzle. Continue blending until uniform. Pour the filling into the prepared crust. Cover with plastic wrap and refrigerate until cold and set, at least 8 hours or up to 24 hours.

NOTE: If desired, garnish the pie with shaved chocolate. Or drizzle slices with chocolate sauce or a little softened but room-temperature Hot Fudge Sauce (page 27).

NUTELLA–RICOTTA PIE

Well, sure, everyone should at least once mix Nutella and ricotta to make a pie. The gelatin will hold it all in place; the banana will give it a great texture. After that, you'll just need whipped cream—mostly to, ahem, cut the richness. • MAKES ONE 9-INCH PIE

1 teaspoon unflavored powdered gelatin

1 tablespoon water

One 15-ounce container whole-milk ricotta cheese (1¾ cups)

1¼ cups Nutella

1 small, very ripe banana, peeled

One 6-ounce purchased chocolate cookie pie crust or one 9-inch homemade Chocolate Sandwich Cookie Crust (page 84)

Turbo Blender Whipped Cream (see page 52) or purchased whipped dairy topping

1. Sprinkle the gelatin over the water in a small, microwave-safe bowl or cup. Set aside until all the water has been absorbed, about 5 minutes.

2. Meanwhile, put the ricotta cheese, Nutella, and banana in the large canister. Cover and blend at the highest speed, stopping the machine repeatedly so you can scrape down the inside of the canister, until very thick and smooth, about 1 minute.

3. Microwave the gelatin mixture on high until melted, about 10 seconds; add it to the ricotta mixture. Cover and blend at the highest speed, again stopping the machine repeatedly to scrape down the inside of the canister, until super thick, about 30 seconds.

4. Scrape and spread into the prepared pie crust. Cover with plastic wrap and refrigerate until cold and set, at least 8 hours or up to 24 hours. To serve, top the pie with whipped cream before slicing into wedges.

PB&J–CREAM CHEESE PIE

We don't need any gelatin here since the peanut butter provides the extra body to give the filling a great, rich texture. We also like this pie in the Vanilla Cookie Crust (page 84). • MAKES ONE 9-INCH PIE

8 ounces regular cream cheese

¾ cup smooth peanut butter

¾ cup heavy cream

½ cup confectioners' sugar

One 6-ounce purchased graham cracker pie crust or one 9-inch homemade Graham Cracker Crust (page 84)

¾ cup strawberry jam

Chopped roasted, salted peanuts, for garnish

1. Put the cream cheese, peanut butter, cream, and confectioners' sugar in the large canister. Cover and blend at the highest speed, turning the machine on and off quite often and scraping down the inside of the canister, until smooth and very thick, 2 to 3 minutes. Scrape and spread the mixture into the prepared pie crust.

2. Warm the jam in a small bowl in the microwave on high until spreadable, about 10 seconds, stirring well. Spread over the top of the pie. Refrigerate the pie until cold and set, at least 4 hours or up to 24 hours. To serve, garnish the top with chopped peanuts before slicing into wedges.

ICEBOX CAKES & CHEESECAKES

O N TO THE SHOWSTOPPERS! THESE CAN IMPRESS COMPANY. (YOU MAY OR MAY NOT WANT TO TELL YOUR FRIENDS AND FAMILY HOW EASY THESE ARE.) YOUR GRANDMOTHER PROBABLY KNOWS MORE ABOUT ICEBOX CAKES THAN YOU DO.

They're like an American version of an English trifle, made by layering a custard between shortbread cookies, ladyfinger cookies, vanilla wafer cookies, in a 9-inch square, *deep-dish*, baking pan (not just a standard 9-inch pan—check out the one in the photo on the opposite page). The cake then needs about 24 hours in the fridge so the cookies can soften to luxurious "layers." Plan on making these cakes the day before you serve them. You can try to cut them into pieces to serve, but since they're quite soft, almost pudding-like, you can also go old school: scoop them up with a big spoon to serve in bowls.

ABOUT THOSE COOKIES

We haven't offered any cookie recipes. We've assumed you'll buy the cookies, just as we did. That said, there's a vast difference in quality among the purchased cookies. Some are fairly tasteless, made with lots of fake flavorings and tasteless fats. Others are more like what you'd make at home. We encourage you to buy the best you can find.

You'll notice throughout that we made a guesstimate of the number of cookies you'll need. Nine-inch pans may all be the same size but not so with the store-bought cookies, which may be thicker, thinner, bigger, or smaller than those we used in testing. So we had to approximate. The point is to create a fairly even layer,

breaking the cookies to fill any large cracks and holes. There's no need to get obsessive; but the fuller the layer, the more successful the ice box cake will be.

There are two kinds of ladyfinger cookies available in North American supermarkets: a hard, crisp cookie and a fairly soft, spongy one. We used the latter throughout this section. They're usually found in the bakery department rather than the cookie aisle. Our supermarket in rural New England had them in the back freezer case at the bakery counter. We had to ask for them. If you can't find the softer ladyfingers, buy a sponge cake or a pound cake and cut it into ½-inch-thick strips to layer in the dessert.

NO-BAKE CHEESECAKES

After the ice box cakes, we turn to the cheesecakes, a real treat from the turbo blender. They're so easy! Just put the ingredients inside, whir them until smooth, and pour the mixture into a prepared crust. There's no baking involved! Because the added lemon juice or other acids can set the dairy (including the cream cheese), and because we use softened gelatin as well, we don't have to worry about water baths or special oven rack settings for these cheesecakes. Best of all, you'll never have to worry about a cheesecake cracking!

LEMON CREAM ICEBOX CAKE

What could be easier? Or better? Here, a rich lemon custard is layered among vanilla cookies, then put it in the refrigerator to set up into a cake. Since both the lemon juice and the butter go into the already steaming mixture, make sure those two ingredients are at room temperature so they don't cool it off and cause it to break at an inopportune moment. Some of the cookies may float to the top of the custard as it sets. Don't worry: these will get covered with whipped cream! • MAKES ONE 9-INCH SQUARE, DEEP-DISH CAKE

2 cups whole milk

1 cup heavy cream

¾ cup granulated white sugar

3 large egg yolks

⅓ cup fresh lemon juice, at room temperature

¼ cup cornstarch

1 tablespoon unsalted butter, at room temperature

¼ teaspoon lemon extract

¼ teaspoon salt, optional

One 11-ounce box vanilla wafer cookies, plus additional for garnish if desired

Turbo Blender Whipped Cream (page 52) or purchased whipped cream

1. Put the milk, cream, sugar, and egg yolks in the large canister. Cover and blend at the highest speed until steaming (about 120°F), approximately 4 minutes.

2. Add the lemon juice, cornstarch, butter, lemon extract, and salt, if using. Cover and blend at the highest speed, venting the lid if necessary, until quite thick and the temperature reaches 170°F, about 2 minutes. Because

of varying moisture content in the egg yolks as well as blade speed, the mixture may thicken before it reaches the peak temperature. Make sure that it is above 160°F for egg safety and a proper set. Do not strain the motor.

3. Lay about a third of the cookies in a 9-inch square, deep-dish, baking pan; top with a third of the custard in the canister. Continue alternating cookies and custard, using equivalent amounts of each to make two more layers, ending with custard on top. Refrigerate for 24 hours, until the cookies have softened and the cake is set, covering with plastic wrap once chilled. To serve, spread whipped cream over the cake. Garnish with additional crumbled cookies, if desired.

NOTE: You can also use bottled lemon juice, but make sure it's not from concentrate or pasteurized.

STRAWBERRY SHORTCAKE ICEBOX CAKE

For the best flavor, look for crisp shortbread cookies, particularly premium ones made with butter. They'll soften into shortcake-like layers between the custard. Do not use frozen berries—once thawed, they're too wet for a good custard set. • MAKES ONE 9-INCH SQUARE, DEEP-DISH CAKE

4 cups sliced, hulled fresh strawberries, plus additional for garnish

1¼ cups granulated white sugar

2 cups whole milk

½ cup heavy cream

2 large eggs, plus 1 large egg yolk

1 tablespoon pure vanilla extract

¼ teaspoon salt, optional

¼ cup cornstarch

About 40 purchased shortbread cookies

Turbo Blender Whipped Cream (page 52) or purchased whipped cream

1. Mix the sliced strawberries and ½ cup of the sugar in a large bowl until the strawberries are well coated in the sugar. Set aside to macerate at room temperature for 30 minutes, stirring occasionally.

2. Put the remaining ¾ cup sugar along with the milk, cream, eggs, egg yolk, vanilla, and salt, if using, in the large canister. Cover and blend at the highest speed until steaming (about 120°F), approximately 4 minutes.

3. Add the cornstarch. Cover and blend at the highest speed, venting the lid if necessary, until fairly well thickened and the temperature reaches 170°F, about 2 minutes.

4. Lay about a third of the shortbread cookies in a 9-inch square, deep-dish baking pan, breaking some cookies to fill any gaps as necessary (without getting too obsessive); top with a third of the pudding mixture in the canister and a third of the macerated strawberries. Repeat this procedure two more times, using equivalent amounts of each of the components to make a total of three layers, ending with macerated strawberries on top. Refrigerate for 24 hours, until the cookies have softened and the cake is set, covering with plastic wrap once chilled. To serve, top the cake with whipped cream and garnish with sliced strawberries.

TIRAMISU ICEBOX CAKE

This easy cake is modeled on a favorite Italian "pick-me-up," traditionally an afternoon treat but equally welcome after a summer barbecue. The standard whipped cream recipe in this book may make a little more than you need for a classic, flat top on this cake. If that doesn't bother you, just pile it all on and give the cake a rounded top. No one will complain.

MAKES ONE 9-INCH SQUARE, DEEP-DISH CAKE

1½ cups whole milk

¾ cup granulated white sugar

6 large egg yolks

2 teaspoons instant coffee powder or instant espresso powder

1 teaspoon pure vanilla extract

¼ teaspoon salt, optional

¼ cup cornstarch

8 ounces mascarpone cheese (see Note)

About 36 purchased ladyfinger cookies

Turbo Blender Whipped Cream (page 52) or purchased whipped cream

Unsweetened cocoa powder, for dusting

1. Put the milk, sugar, egg yolks, instant coffee or espresso powder, vanilla, and salt, if using, in the large canister. Cover and blend at the highest speed until steaming (about 120°F), approximately 4 minutes.

2. Add the cornstarch. Cover and blend at the highest speed, venting the lid if necessary, until fairly well thickened and the temperature reaches 170°F, about 2 minutes. Add the mascarpone cheese and blend at low speed until smooth, about 20 seconds.

3. To build the cake, place about 12 lady-finger cookies in a 9-inch square, deep-dish baking pan, breaking some cookies to fill in any gaps. Top with a third of the custard in the canister. Repeat two more times, using equivalent amounts of each component for the layers to make a total of three layers that end with the custard on top. Refrigerate for 24 hours, until the cookies have softened and the cake is set, covering with plastic wrap once chilled. To serve, spread whipped cream over the chilled cake and dust with cocoa powder.

NOTE: Mascarpone is a soft cheese, rather like a creamier version of cream cheese. You'll find it at the cheese counter of most large supermarkets.

WHITE CHOCOLATE–GINGERSNAP ICEBOX CAKE

Make sure you use gingersnap cookies with that decided "snap" of ginger, nothing wimpy to stand up to the white chocolate custard. Check those packages of white chocolate, too. Some white chocolate is little more than flavored vegetable shortening. If possible, buy the real thing. • MAKES ONE 9-INCH SQUARE, DEEP-DISH CAKE

2½ cups whole milk

¾ cup heavy cream

6 ounces white chocolate, broken into squares or roughly chopped

2 large egg yolks

2 teaspoons pure vanilla extract

¼ teaspoon salt

¼ cup cornstarch

1¼ cups orange marmalade

About 40 gingersnap cookies

Turbo Blender Whipped Cream (see page 52) or purchased whipped dairy topping

1. Put the milk, cream, white chocolate, egg yolks, vanilla, and salt in the large canister. Cover and blend at the highest speed until steaming (about 120°F), approximately 4 minutes.

2. Add the cornstarch. Cover and blend at the highest speed, venting the lid if necessary, until fairly well thickened and the temperature reaches 170°F, about 2 minutes.

3. Put the marmalade in a small, microwave-safe bowl. Microwave on high until spreadable, 10 to 15 seconds, stirring after every 5 seconds.

4. To build the cake, place about 10 gingersnap cookies on the bottom of a 9-inch square, deep-dish baking pan, breaking some to fill in the gaps or make a more even layer. Spread ¼ cup of the marmalade over them, then pour and spread a quarter of the custard evenly on top. Repeat this process three more times, using equivalent amounts of the components each time, to create a total of four layers that end with the custard on top. You will have ¼ cup marmalade left over; cover and set aside at room temperature. Refrigerate the cake for 24 hours, until the cookies have softened and the cake is set, covering with plastic wrap once chilled.

5. To serve, warm the leftover marmalade for about 5 seconds on high in the microwave, just until spreadable but not hot. Stir well. Top the cake with the whipped cream, then drizzle the softened marmalade on top.

CHOCOLATE, BANANA, AND PEANUT BUTTER ICEBOX CAKE

This one's like the best peanut butter cake—with chocolate in the mix! And if you want to go all out, turn it into an Elvis cake by crumbling crisp bacon bits over the chocolate whipped cream just before serving. Don't say we didn't warn you. • MAKES ONE 9-INCH SQUARE, DEEP-DISH CAKE

2¾ cups heavy cream

2½ cups whole milk

1 cup granulated white sugar

½ cup peanut butter (of any sort)

1 large egg

2½ teaspoons pure vanilla extract

¼ cup cornstarch

About 48 chocolate wafer cookies

4 large, very ripe bananas, peeled and thinly sliced

¼ cup confectioners' sugar

3 tablespoons unsweetened cocoa powder

1. Put ¾ cup of the cream, the milk, granulated white sugar, peanut butter, egg, and 2 teaspoons of the vanilla in the large canister. Cover and blend at the highest speed until steaming (about 120°F), approximately 4 minutes.

2. Add the cornstarch. Cover and blend at the highest speed, venting the lid if necessary, until quite thick and the temperature reaches 160°F, about 1 minute.

3. To build the cake, place about 12 chocolate wafer cookies in the bottom of a 9-inch square, deep-dish baking pan, breaking some of the cookies to fill some of the gaps and make as even a layer as possible. Top with a quarter of the banana slices and then a quarter of the custard in the canister. Repeat this process three more times, using equivalent amounts of the components each time, to create a total of four layers that end with the custard on top. Refrigerate for 24 hours, until the cookies have softened and the cake is set, covering with plastic wrap once chilled.

4. Clean and dry the canister. Add the remaining 2 cups cream, the remaining ½ teaspoon vanilla, the confectioners' sugar, and cocoa. Cover and blend at the highest speed until thickened like whipped cream, just a few seconds, and no more than 20 seconds. Spread over the top of the cake just before serving.

BANANAS FOSTER ICEBOX CAKE

The classic New Orleans dessert of bananas, caramel, and (lots of) butter just got turned into an icebox cake! Use soft, ripe bananas. You want lots of flavor to stand up to all that caramel sauce in the custard. • MAKES ONE 9-INCH SQUARE, DEEP-DISH CAKE

6 tablespoons (¾ stick) unsalted butter

4 large, very ripe bananas, peeled and thinly sliced

6 tablespoons packed dark brown sugar

1⅓ cups whole milk

⅔ cup heavy cream

⅔ cup purchased caramel sauce

3 tablespoons packed light brown sugar

2 large egg yolks

2 teaspoons pure vanilla extract

2½ tablespoons cornstarch

About 42 purchased ladyfinger cookies

Turbo Blender Whipped Cream (see page 52) or purchased whipped dairy topping

1. Melt 4 tablespoons (½ stick) of the butter in a large skillet set over medium heat. Add the bananas and cook, stirring gently, until lightly browned and softened, about 2 minutes. Sprinkle the dark brown sugar on top; cook, stirring very gently, until the sugar melts and coats the bananas, about 1 minute. Remove from the heat and set aside.

2. Put the milk, cream, caramel sauce, light brown sugar, egg yolks, and vanilla in the large canister. Cover and blend at the highest speed until steaming, about 4 minutes.

3. Add the cornstarch and the remaining 2 tablespoons butter. Cover and blend at the highest speed, venting the lid if necessary, until fairly well thickened and the temperature reaches 170°F, about 2 minutes.

4. To build the cake, place about half the ladyfingers in the bottom of a 9-inch square, deep-dish baking pan, breaking a few of the cookies to make as even a layer as possible and filling in some of the gaps. Top with half of the banana slices in the skillet and half of the custard in the canister. Repeat once more, ending with the custard on top. Refrigerate for 24 hours, until the cookies have softened and the cake is set, covering with plastic wrap once chilled. To serve, spread whipped cream over the cake.

CHOCOLATE-RASPBERRY ICEBOX CAKE

This one's fancy enough for company, especially if you decorate the top with more fresh raspberries. If you don't want any alcohol in the final product (it won't all "cook out"), use raspberry-flavored syrup, such as one made by Torani or Monin. • MAKES ONE 9-INCH SQUARE, DEEP-DISH CAKE

4 cups fresh raspberries (about 1 pound), plus more for garnishing if desired

1¼ cups granulated white sugar

1 tablespoon fresh lemon juice

2½ cups whole milk

¾ cup heavy cream

½ cup unsweetened cocoa powder

¼ cup raspberry liqueur, such as Chambord, or raspberry syrup

1 large egg

¼ cup cornstarch

1 tablespoon unsalted butter

One 14.4-ounce box graham crackers (see Note)

Turbo Blender Whipped Cream (page 52) or purchased whipped cream

1. Mix the fresh raspberries, ¼ cup of the sugar, and the lemon juice in a large bowl. Mash the raspberries lightly against the sides of the bowl just to break them up a bit. Set aside to macerate at room temperature for 20 minutes, stirring occasionally.

2. Put the remaining 1 cup sugar, the milk, cream, cocoa powder, raspberry liqueur or syrup, and egg in the large canister. Cover and blend at the highest speed until steaming (about 120°F), approximately 4 minutes.

3. Add the cornstarch and butter. Cover and blend at the highest speed, venting the lid if necessary, until quite thick and the temperature reaches 170°F, about 2 minutes.

4. To build the cake, place about a quarter of the graham crackers evenly across the bottom of a 9-inch square, deep-dish baking pan, breaking the cookies to make them fit into an even layer. Top with a quarter of the raspberry mixture and then a quarter of the custard in the canister. Repeat this process three more times, using equivalent amounts of the components each time, to make a total of four layers that end with the custard. Refrigerate for 24 hours, until the cookies have softened and the cake is set, covering with plastic wrap once chilled.

5. To serve, spread whipped cream over the top of the cold cake. Garnish with additional fresh raspberries, if desired.

NOTE: For more intense chocolate flavor, use chocolate-flavored graham crackers (not chocolate-coated graham crackers).

CHERRY-VANILLA NO-BAKE CHEESECAKE

Here's an easy cheesecake that would be welcome at a summer picnic or a winter meal. You'll need a 9-inch round springform pan because we'll make this one "old school" with a traditional graham cracker crust that you press right into the pan. Since it's a no-bake crust, you'll want to serve the cheesecake slightly chilled, no more than 15 minutes out of the fridge. Otherwise, the crust can start to fall apart as the butter softens to room temperature. • MAKES ONE 9-INCH ROUND CHEESECAKE

1½ cups graham cracker crumbs

½ cup walnut pieces

¼ cup granulated white sugar

6 tablespoons (¾ stick) unsalted butter, melted and cooled, plus additional for greasing the pan

1 teaspoon powdered unflavored gelatin

1 tablespoon water

1 pound regular cream cheese, at room temperature

2 cups vanilla whole-milk Greek yogurt (see Note)

⅔ cup confectioners' sugar

2 tablespoons fresh lime juice (see Note)

1 cup canned cherry pie filling

1. Lightly butter the inside of a 9-inch round springform pan or a high-sided cheesecake pan.

2. Place the graham cracker crumbs, walnuts, and granulated white sugar in the large canister; pulse a couple of times to blend. Add the melted butter, cover, and pulse to combine until uniform. Pour and scrape the mixture into the prepared pan. Press and smooth the mixture with your clean, dry fingers to form an even crust across the bottom and halfway up the sides of the pan.

3. Sprinkle the gelatin over the water in a small microwave-safe bowl or cup. Set aside until the liquid has been absorbed, about 5 minutes.

4. Wash and dry the canister. Add the cream cheese, yogurt, confectioners' sugar, and lime juice. Cover and blend at the highest speed until smooth, stopping the machine repeatedly to scrape down the inside of the canister, just a few seconds and no more than 20 seconds.

5. Warm the gelatin mixture in the microwave on high until melted, about 10 seconds. Add to the cream cheese mixture, cover, and blend at the highest speed until very thick and smooth, again stopping the machine repeatedly to scrape down the inside of the canister, about 20 seconds.

6. Pour and spread the filling into the prepared crust. Refrigerate until set, about 8 hours or up to 24 hours, covering with plastic wrap once chilled.

7. To serve, let the cheesecake sit out at room temperature for about 10 minutes. Loosen and remove the side of the pan, if using a springform pan. Top the cheesecake with the cherry pie filling before slicing into wedges to serve.

NOTE: Use only whole-milk Greek yogurt, not fat-free. And you *must* use fresh lime juice to get the proper set.

MINT CHOCOLATE NO-BAKE CHEESECAKE

Rather than a ribbon of chocolate in a mint cheesecake, we use the turbo blender to create an ultra-smooth, almost velvety, no-bake cheesecake. Of course, if you are so inclined, you can just omit the mint extract to make a more straightforward chocolate cheesecake. However, it will be a rather pale brown. So just drizzle the slices with more chocolate syrup. • MAKES ONE 9-INCH ROUND CHEESECAKE

Nonstick cooking spray

20 chocolate sandwich cookies, such as Oreos or Hydrox

4 tablespoons (½ stick) unsalted butter, melted and cooled

One ¼-ounce package unflavored powdered gelatin

1½ tablespoons water

1½ pounds regular cream cheese, at room temperature

1 cup chocolate syrup

¾ cup regular sour cream

6 tablespoons granulated white sugar

1¼ teaspoons mint extract

1. Lightly coat the inside of a 9-inch-round springform pan or a high-sided cheesecake pan with nonstick cooking spray.

2. Put the cookies in the large canister; cover and blend at low speed until finely ground. Dump these crumbs into a large bowl and stir in the butter until evenly moistened. Pour the mixture into the prepared pan. Using your clean, dry fingers, press the mixture into an even crust across the bottom of the pan and 1½ inches up the side.

3. Mix the gelatin and water in a small, microwave-safe bowl. Set aside until all the liquid has been absorbed, about 5 minutes.

4. Meanwhile, wipe out the large canister. Add the cream cheese, chocolate syrup, sour cream, sugar, and mint extract. Cover and blend at low speed until smooth, stopping the machine repeatedly to scrape down the inside of the canister, 1 minute.

5. Microwave the gelatin mixture on high for 10 seconds to melt. Add it to the blender, cover, and blend at low speed until smooth. Pour the filling into the prepared crust. Refrigerate until set, about 8 hours or up to 24 hours, covering with plastic wrap once chilled.

6. To serve, let the cheesecake sit out at room temperature for about 10 minutes. Loosen and remove the side of the pan, if using a springform pan. Cut into wedges to serve.

ORANGE NO-BAKE CHEESECAKE

For the best flavor in this light, creamy cheesecake, use freshly squeezed orange juice. There's no need to strain out the pulp since the blender will make short work of it.

MAKES ONE 9-INCH ROUND CHEESECAKE

1½ cups vanilla wafer cookies, crumbled (purchased or ground from 12 –16 cookies)

½ cup sliced almonds

¼ teaspoon ground cinnamon

6 tablespoons (¾ stick) unsalted butter, melted and cooled, plus additional for greasing the pan

1 teaspoon powdered unflavored gelatin

¼ cup fresh orange juice

1 pound regular cream cheese, at room temperature

One 14-ounce can regular sweetened condensed whole milk

½ cup orange marmalade

1 teaspoon orange extract

Thin strips of candied orange zest, optional, for garnish

1. Lightly butter the inside of a 9-inch round springform pan or a high-sided cheesecake pan.

2. Put the cookie crumbs, almonds, and cinnamon in the large canister. Pulse a couple of times to combine. Add the butter, cover, and pulse a few times until uniform. Pour the mixture into the prepared pan. Using your clean, dry fingers, press it into an even crust across the bottom and halfway up the sides of the pan.

3. Sprinkle the gelatin over the orange juice in a small, microwave-safe bowl. Set aside to soften for 5 minutes.

4. Wash and dry the canister. Add the cream cheese, sweetened condensed milk, marmalade, and orange extract. Cover and blend at the highest speed until smooth, stopping the machine repeatedly to scrape down the inside of the canister, about 30 seconds.

5. Warm the gelatin mixture in the microwave on high until melted, about 10 seconds. Pour into the cream cheese mixture, cover, and blend at the highest speed, stopping the machine repeatedly to scrape down the inside of the canister, until smooth, about 30 seconds.

6. Pour and spread the filling into the prepared crust. Refrigerate until set, for at least 8 hours or up to 48 hours, covering with plastic wrap once chilled.

7. To serve, let the cheesecake sit out at room temperature for 10 to 15 minutes. Unfasten and remove the sides of the springform pan, if using. Top with candied orange zest as a garnish, if desired, before slicing the cheesecake into wedges.

NOTE: If you want to make a boozy cheesecake, substitute Triple Sec or even Cointreau for the orange juice.

PEANUT BUTTER NO-BAKE CHEESECAKE WITH A CHOCOLATE GLAZE

If you'd rather not drizzle chocolate over the cheesecake, soften a little strawberry or raspberry jam in the same way in the microwave, then cool it a bit and spread it in an even layer on the cake for a quick glaze.

MAKES ONE 9-INCH ROUND CHEESECAKE

1 cup roasted unsalted peanuts

1 cup graham cracker crumbs

2 tablespoons granulated white sugar

2 tablespoons unsalted butter, melted and cooled, plus additional for greasing the pan

1 pound regular cream cheese, at room temperature

1½ cups smooth peanut butter

⅔ cup regular sour cream or whole-milk Greek yogurt

1 tablespoon pure vanilla extract

2 cups confectioners' sugar

¾ cup purchased hot fudge sauce or homemade Hot Fudge Sauce (page 27)

2 tablespoons heavy cream

1. Lightly butter the inside of a 9-inch round springform pan or a high-sided cheesecake pan.

2. Put the peanuts, graham cracker crumbs, and granulated white sugar in the large canister. Pulse a couple of times to combine. Add the butter, cover, and blend at low speed until uniform and moist, about 10 seconds. Pour this mixture into the prepared pan. Using clean, dry fingers, press it into an even crust across the bottom and halfway up the sides of the pan.

3. Clean and dry the canister. Add the cream cheese, peanut butter, sour cream or Greek yogurt, and vanilla. Cover and blend at the highest speed until smooth, stopping the machine repeatedly to scrape down the inside of the canister, about 30 seconds.

4. Add the confectioners' sugar, cover, and blend at the highest speed, stopping the machine repeatedly to scrape down the inside of the canister, until smooth and quite thick, less than 1 minute.

5. Pour and scrape the filling into the prepared crust. Refrigerate until set, at least 8 hours or up to 48 hours, covering with plastic wrap once chilled.

6. Just before serving, put the hot fudge sauce in a small, microwave-safe bowl. Warm in the microwave on high in 10-second bursts, stirring after each, until smooth but not hot. Stir in the cream. Cool for 2 minutes. Unlatch and remove the sides of the springform pan, if using. Spread and smooth the chocolate mixture over the cheesecake before slicing into wedges to serve.

PINEAPPLE CHEESECAKE

A no-bake cheesecake won't set with fresh pineapple in the mix, so we used canned pineapple but then bumped up the flavor with pineapple jam. The results are silky smooth. If you're serving this for the holidays, you could top with glacéed fruit once it has set in the refrigerator. • MAKES ONE 9-INCH ROUND CHEESECAKE

Nonstick cooking spray

40 vanilla wafer cookies

2 tablespoons granulated white sugar

4 tablespoons (½ stick) unsalted butter, melted and cooled

¼ cup pineapple juice (drained from an 8-ounce can of crushed pineapple—see below)

I teaspoon unflavored powdered gelatin

I pound regular cream cheese, at room temperature

I cup pineapple jam

¼ cup, drained, canned crushed pineapple

¼ cup regular sour cream

2 tablespoons packed light brown sugar

1. Lightly coat the inside of a 9-inch round springform pan or a high-sided cheesecake pan with nonstick cooking spray.

2. Put the cookies and granulated white sugar in the large canister; cover and blend at low speed until finely ground, about 10 seconds. Pour into a large bowl and stir in the melted butter until evenly moistened. Pour this mixture into the prepared pan. Using your clean, dry fingers, press the mixture into an even crust across the bottom of the pan and 1 inch up the sides.

3. Stir the pineapple juice and gelatin together in a small, microwave-safe bowl. Set aside to soften the gelatin for 5 minutes.

4. Wipe out the large canister. Add the cream cheese, pineapple jam, crushed pineapple, sour cream, and brown sugar. Cover and blend at high speed until thick and creamy, stopping the machine repeatedly to scrape down the inside of the canister, about 1 minute.

5. Microwave the gelatin mixture on high for 10 seconds to melt the gelatin, then add it to the large canister. Cover and blend on low speed until smooth, about 20 seconds.

6. Pour and scrape the filling gently into the prepared pan, so as not to dislodge the crust. Refrigerate until set, about 8 hours or up to 24 hours, covering with plastic wrap once chilled.

7. To serve, let the cheesecake sit out at room temperature for about 10 minutes. Loosen and remove the side of the pan, if using a springform pan. Slice into wedges to serve.

FIVE CRUSTS

IF YOU WANT TO GO ALL OUT, YOU'LL MAKE CRUSTS FOR YOUR CREAM PIES. CONSIDER THESE A MIX-AND-MATCH AFFAIR. WHILE WE'VE given suggestions in the pie chapter for the best crust with a certain filling, we've done so based on our tastes or traditional fits (a graham cracker crust with a banana cream pie, for example). *You* shouldn't feel the need to stand on ceremony. Why not try a coconut crust with that banana cream filling?

These are all no-bake crusts, fairly easy to pull together when you're in a rush. However, none will be as firm as a baked crust—and all will need to stay a bit chilled for them to hold together under the filling. But if you want a firmer graham cracker or vanilla cookie crust, form the crust in the plate as directed, then bake at 325°F for 10 minutes or until set. Cool to room temperature on a wire rack before filling.

GRAHAM CRACKER CRUST

Of course you can make this crust with purchased graham cracker crumbs, as written here. But since you've got that high-powered blender on the countertop, you might as well use it. You'll need ten to twelve whole graham crackers to make the necessary amount of crumbs. • MAKES ONE 9-INCH PIE CRUST

1½ cups graham cracker crumbs

¼ cup packed light brown sugar

½ teaspoon ground cinnamon

¼ teaspoon salt, optional

7 tablespoons unsalted butter, melted and cooled

1. Mix the graham cracker crumbs, sugar, cinnamon, and salt, if using, in a large bowl until uniform. Add the melted butter and stir until moist and uniform. Pour into a 9-inch pie plate.

2. Using your clean, dry fingers, press the mixture into an even crust across the bottom and up the sides of the pie plate. Cover with plastic wrap and refrigerate for 1 hour or up to 24 hours before using.

VANILLA COOKIE CRUST

If you want to get ready for the summer weekends or holidays, make several of these crusts in disposable tins, then cover and store in the freezer for up to 4 months. Since vanilla cookies come in all sorts of shapes, it's hard to determine just how many you'll need in the blender to make the crumbs yourself.

But figure on three cups of roughly broken cookies for the right amount. • MAKES ONE 9-INCH PIE CRUST

2 cups vanilla cookie crumbs, such as Nilla Wafer crumbs

8 tablespoons (1 stick) unsalted butter, melted and cooled

⅓ cup confectioners' sugar

1. Mix the cookie crumbs, melted butter, and confectioners' sugar in a large bowl until moist and uniform. Pour into a 9-inch pie plate.

2. Using your clean, dry fingers, press the mixture into an even crust across the bottom and up the sides of the pie plate. Cover with plastic wrap and refrigerate for 1 hour or up to 24 hours before using.

CHOCOLATE SANDWICH COOKIE CRUST

No, we're not talking about those small, round, chocolate cookies often used in chocolate crusts. We're talking about stuffed sandwich cookies. Now *those* can make a crust! For the right proportions, don't use either double-stuffed or half-stuffed Oreos. MAKES ONE 9-INCH PIE CRUST

16 chocolate sandwich cookies, such as Oreo or Hydrox cookies (see headnote)

6 tablespoons (¾ stick) unsalted butter, melted and cooled

¼ cup confectioners' sugar

1. Place the cookies in the large canister. Cover and pulse until ground to fine crumbs. Pour into a large bowl; add the melted butter and confectioners' sugar and stir until moist and uniform. Pour into a 9-inch pie plate.

2. Using your clean, dry fingers, press the mixture into an even crust across the bottom and up the sides of the pie plate. Cover with plastic wrap and refrigerate for at least 2 hours or up to 24 hours before using.

COCONUT CRUST

The bread crumbs give this crust its body and snap, something coconut alone won't provide. Note that this recipe calls for *unsweetened* shredded coconut. The sweetened stuff is too sticky to make a good crust with the right texture. • MAKES ONE 9-INCH PIE CRUST

1½ cups unsweetened shredded coconut

½ cup confectioners' sugar

½ cup plain dried bread crumbs

5 tablespoons (½ stick plus 1 tablespoon) unsalted butter, melted and cooled

1. Place the coconut and confectioners' sugar in the large canister. Cover and blend at the highest speed until finely ground, about 10 seconds. Pour into a large bowl. Add the bread crumbs and melted butter; stir until moist and uniform. Pour into a 9-inch pie plate.

2. Using your clean, dry fingers, press the mixture into an even crust across the bottom and up the sides of the pie plate. Cover with plastic wrap and refrigerate for at least 2 hours or up to 24 hours before using.

SALTY PRETZEL CRUST

If you like salt the way we do, you'll get hooked on this crust, a great treat under many of our cream pies. • MAKES ONE 9-INCH PIE CRUST

3½ cups pretzel nuggets

8 tablespoons (1 stick) unsalted butter, melted and cooled

⅓ cup packed light brown sugar

1. Put the pretzel nuggets in the large canister. Cover and pulse repeatedly until finely ground. Pour into a large bowl. Add the melted butter and sugar; stir until moist and uniform. Pour into a 9-inch pie plate.

2. Using your clean, dry fingers, press the mixture into an even crust across the bottom and up the sides of the pie plate. Cover with plastic wrap and refrigerate for at least 2 hours or up to 24 hours before using.

CAKES, CRISPS, COBBLERS, & MORE

HAVE YOU EVER WANTED TO RUN A BAKERY? NEITHER HAVE WE. BUT BOY, WE SURE LIKE LAYER CAKES, SCONES, AND BROWNIES. THESE ARE AMERICAN CLASSICS, DESSERTS THAT HAVE BEEN AROUND FOR GENERATIONS AND PLEASED MILLIONS.

WE'RE NOT GOING TO REINVENT THE WHEEL (OR THE BROWNIE, AS THE CASE MAY BE). WE ARE GOING TO MAKE ALL THESE BAKED TREATS A LOT SIMPLER. (AND A LITTLE HEALTHIER, TOO, AS YOU'LL SEE.) NOW THAT WE'VE GOT A TURBO BLENDER, WE CAN WHIP UP BATTERS, COBBLER TOPPINGS, AND LIGHT DESSERT SAUCES IN MINUTES, SOMETIMES IN SECONDS.

THE THICKER THE BATTER . . . .

Most baking recipes for turbo blenders encourage you to make the flour in the blender but leave most of the rest of the recipe for subsequent steps in a bowl on the countertop. Not ours! We're doing as much of the recipe in the canister as we can.

However, we sometimes use that extra bowl, particularly for super-thick batters that could strain the motor. But even in these, we've created a hybrid technique that requires less work. First, we grind the flour and other dry ingredients in the canister, then dump that mixture into a bowl. Next, we whir the eggs and liquid ingredients in the same canister and dump it in the same bowl. We stir it together and we're done.

Notwithstanding the exceptions, many of these recipes are far simpler: we do the whole thing, dry to liquid, right in the canister in one shot. Done!

Even so, a batter is thicker than a custard. We have to make accommodations, which we've covered in the introduction: either use the tamper, if available, or stop the machine repeatedly to reposition the ingredients. Although it may seem obvious, it's worth stating up front: don't ever stick a rubber spatula or the handle of a wooden spoon (or anything else!) in a turbo blender while it's running.

We should add that getting the batter out of the blender canister is sticky work. The batter will be caught in the corners, along the seams, and around the blades. You'll need a long-handled narrow rubber spatula and some patience. Try to scrape out as much as you can. You needn't get every speck but you don't want to waste this tasty treat.

MORE ABOUT WHEAT BERRIES

Throughout, we begin by grinding soft white wheat berries to a fine flour. For more information on wheat berries, see page 3. But we should say something here about the grinding process itself. The blender will heat the grains as they're ground. You shouldn't let the flour go so long that it gets hot. Nevertheless, it will warm up. You may notice some sticking to the bottom of the lid. If so, take the canister off the motor housing and rap it, covered, against the countertop a couple of times to knock the flour free and back down into the mix. If it's really stuck, use a rubber spatula to get as much off as you can.

We're looking to grind the grains into what we repeatedly call a "fine flour." We mean a flour that doesn't feel coarse between your fingers but much like all-purpose flour. There will be tiny bits of brown in it because—huzzah!—we're making whole grain treats from wheat berries.

We told you: healthier. *Every* dessert in this section is a whole grain dessert. Shhhh, we won't tell if you don't. You'll be serving your friends and family some lovely layer cakes and some crazy-good sheet cakes—and yes, they'll be eating whole grains. Have another brownie!

Because wheat berries have their bran and germ still intact, they can go rancid. Once you get them home, store them in a cool, dark pantry for a month or two. If you're not going to use them that quickly, store them, tightly sealed, in the freezer. There's no need to thaw them for these recipes.

GREASING THE PAN

We often ask you to butter (or grease) and then flour the baking pans. To butter a pan, put a little butter on a piece of wax paper or a paper towel, then run it around the inside of the pan, paying special attention to the corners and seams. To oil a pan, fold a paper towel in quarters, pour a little oil on it, and rub it around the inside of pan, again taking care with those corners and seams.

To flour the pan once it's buttered or oiled, add a little all-purpose flour, no more than 2 tablespoons, then tip the pan this way and that to coat it evenly with a fine film. Tap any excess flour into the sink. If you see spots that have no flour, you may need to grease them again and add a little more flour to get them coated.

BAKING IN GLASS

Glass and Pyrex vessels are terrific insulators—which means they hold heat more efficiently than metal pans. If you're using glass baking pans, reduce the stated temperature by 25°F and the stated time by about 10 percent (this latter is a bald approximation). Watch carefully to make sure you don't overbake the dessert. It will continue to cook in the insulated glass even as it sits, on a wire rack. And grease a glass pan well. Baked goods have a greater tendency to stick to glass.

So that's about it. You're about to discover even more reasons why that high-horsepower, high-rpm blender is one of the most useful tools in your kitchen. And you're about to enjoy some pretty fine baked goods. It all sounds like a win-win to us!

BROWNIES, BLONDIES, & CAKES

HERE'S THE BASIC FORMULA FOR ALMOST ALL OUR BAKED TREATS

Baking classics got their reputation honestly. We can never get enough! And now that they're even easier, we're really in trouble. Thank goodness a turbo blender also turns them into whole-grain treats. We feel better already. So here is the method for almost every one of these recipes.

1. Grind some wheat berries to a fine flour in the large canister.

2. Then either:
    Add the other ingredients directly to the canister to make an easy batter.
        OR
    Pour the flour and other dry ingredients into a bowl and whir together the liquid ingredients in the same canister before stirring the liquid mixture into the flour mixture in the bowl.

If a recipe asks you to make a batter in the slightly more elaborate process—like in the second choice in step 2 above—there's no need to clean the canister between the two steps. So what if a little flour gets into the wet ingredients? It's about to get all mixed together anyway!

ROOM TEMPERATURE INGREDIENTS

In many of these recipes, the eggs and sometimes even the milk and other dairy products *must not be cold*. These ingredients are added later than they were in our pudding, custard, and pie recipes. These are most often added right along with the melted butter. Cold ingredients can quickly chill that butter, causing little bits of it to fall out of suspension.

To get an egg to room temperature, set it on the countertop, still in its shell, for 20 to 25 minutes. Or crack the egg (or eggs—or just the yolks, if the recipe requires it) into a small bowl and set them on the countertop for 10 to 15 minutes. If you're really pressed for time, fill a bowl with warm (not hot!) water and submerge the eggs, still in their shells, in the water for 3 to 5 minutes.

As for the dairy products like milk or sour cream, put these on the countertop for about 20 minutes in their measuring vessels. Or microwave milk (but not sour cream!) on high for no more than 15 seconds.

ARMED WITH THESE FACTS, let's get that blender going! We've got blondies, polenta cakes, buckles, and Bundts to make!

FUDGY BROWNIES

If you like intense, chewy brownies, you've come to the right place. (Just don't tell anyone they're whole grain!) There's a ton of cocoa powder here, weighing down the batter and turning it dense. If you like really fudgy brownies, make sure you underbake them by a minute or two. But in no case should you ever bake these until a toothpick comes out clean! • MAKES 18 TO 24 BROWNIES

1¼ cups soft white wheat berries

¾ cup unsweetened cocoa powder

1 teaspoon baking powder

½ teaspoon salt

1 cup granulated white sugar

1 cup packed light brown sugar

16 tablespoons (2 sticks) unsalted butter, melted and cooled to room temperature, plus additional for greasing the pan

4 large eggs, at room temperature

1 tablespoon pure vanilla extract

1. Position the rack in the center of the oven; heat the oven to 350°F. Lightly but evenly butter the inside of a 9 x 13-inch baking pan.

2. Put the wheat berries in the large canister; cover and blend at the highest speed to a fine flour, about 1 minute. Add the cocoa powder, baking powder, and salt; cover and pulse until evenly combined. Pour this mixture into a large bowl.

3. Put the granulated white sugar, brown sugar, melted butter, eggs, and vanilla in the large canister. Cover and blend at low speed until smooth, less than 1 minute.

4. Pour this mixture into the flour mixture and stir with a wooden spoon until evenly combined with no dry pockets of flour anywhere. Pour and scrape the grainy, thick batter into the prepared pan.

5. Bake until a toothpick or cake tester inserted into the center of the cake comes out *with a few moist crumbs attached*, about 22 minutes. Cool in the pan on a wire rack for 30 minutes. If desired, turn the cake and pan upside down on a cutting board, remove the pan, and then invert the cake again, still on its cutting board, onto a serving platter or a second cutting board. Slice into squares to serve.

NOTE: This batter will never be silky smooth. It will be thick and still a little grainy. Stir it together with a wooden spoon. The undissolved sugar will melt as the brownies bake, rendering them fudgier.

CHOCOLATE SYRUP BROWNIES

Not everyone loves fudgy brownies. There's a cakey crowd out there. We add a little all-purpose flour here to smooth out the consistency and give the brownies more loft. These freeze well: cut them into squares and store between sheets of wax paper in a sealed, plastic container. • MAKES 12 TO 16 BROWNIES

1 cup soft white wheat berries

⅔ cup granulated white sugar

½ teaspoon baking powder

½ teaspoon salt

1 cup chocolate syrup, such as Hershey's or Fox's U-bet

10 tablespoons (1 stick plus 2 tablespoons) unsalted butter, melted and cooled to room temperature, plus additional for greasing the pan

2 large eggs, at room temperature

2 teaspoons pure vanilla extract

2 tablespoons all-purpose flour

1. Position the rack in the center of the oven; heat the oven to 350°F. Use a little butter to grease the inside of a 9-inch square baking pan generously.

2. Put the wheat berries in the large canister; cover and blend at the highest speed to a fine flour, about 1 minute. Add the sugar, baking powder, and salt; cover and pulse to combine. Pour the wheat berry mixture into a large bowl.

3. Put the chocolate syrup, melted butter, eggs, and vanilla in the large canister. Cover and blend at the low speed until smooth, about 10 seconds. Pour over the wheat berry mixture, add the all-purpose flour, and whisk until smooth. Pour and spread the batter into the prepared pan.

4. Bake until the top feels set and a toothpick or cake tester inserted into the center of the cake comes out *with a few moist crumbs attached*, about 25 minutes. Cool in the pan on a wire rack for at least 30 minutes. If desired, turn the cake and pan upside down on a cutting board, remove the pan, and then invert the cake again, still on its cutting board, onto a serving platter or a second cutting board. Slice into squares to serve.

GLUTEN-FREE BROWNIES

We almost didn't label these as "gluten-free." Not because there's any gluten in them but because we wanted everyone to make them! They're rich, dense, and incredibly fudgy, sort of like a flourless chocolate cake but with more chocolate and a better crumb, as befits a brownie. Bring them to a party or the office and don't say a word about "gluten-free." You'll be astounded by the reactions.

MAKES ABOUT 9 BROWNIES

6 tablespoons (¾ stick) unsalted butter, cut into small bits, plus more for greasing the pan

10 ounces semisweet chocolate chips or semisweet chocolate, broken into squares or roughly chopped

¾ cup granulated white sugar

3 large eggs

2 teaspoons pure vanilla extract

⅓ cup cornstarch

¼ cup unsweetened cocoa powder

½ teaspoon ground cinnamon

½ teaspoon salt

1 cup shelled pecan or walnut pieces, roughly chopped

1. Position the rack in the center of the oven; heat the oven to 350°F. Generously butter the inside of an 8-inch square *nonstick* baking pan. Line the bottom of the pan with parchment paper, then butter the parchment paper.

2. Put the butter and chocolate chips or chopped chocolate in a medium, microwave-safe bowl. Microwave on high in 10-second bursts until about three-quarters melted, stirring after each burst. Remove the bowl from the microwave oven and stir until melted and smooth. Set aside at room temperature for 15 minutes.

3. Put the sugar, eggs, and vanilla in the large canister. Cover and blend at the highest speed until smooth and airy, about 1 minute. Add the butter mixture; cover and blend at the highest speed until smooth, about 20 seconds.

4. Add the cornstarch, cocoa powder, cinnamon, and salt. Scrape down the inside of the canister. Cover and blend at low speed, repeatedly stopping the machine to scrape down the inside of the canister with a rubber spatula and reposition the ingredients, or using the tamper, if available, until uniform and smooth, about 30 seconds. The batter will be quite thick. Remove the canister from the power housing, add the nuts, and fold into the batter with a rubber spatula.

5. Scrape and spread the thick batter into the prepared pan, taking care not to dislodge the parchment paper. Bake until set with the characteristic crackly crust and until a cake tester or toothpick inserted into the cake comes out *with a few moist crumbs*, about 35 minutes. Cool in the pan on a wire rack for 10 minutes; then turn the cake out of the pan, peel off the parchment paper, invert onto a cutting board, and continue cooling for 5 minutes or to room temperature.

NOTE: Since these brownies must be baked in a nonstick pan, use only approved cookware like a nonstick-safe spatula to loosen the sides of the brownie cake from the pan.

CHOCOLATE-RASPBERRY BROWNIES

These brownies are a halfway point between fudgy and cakey. We use melted chocolate to keep the batter from becoming too stiff for even a turbo blender. To melt the chocolate, set it in a microwave-safe bowl and microwave on high in 10-second bursts, stirring until it is almost all melted. Remove from the microwave and continue to stir until smooth. Cool for at least 15 minutes at room temperature.

MAKES 12 TO 16 BROWNIES

¾ cup soft white wheat berries

¾ cup granulated white sugar

½ teaspoon baking soda

½ teaspoon salt

10 tablespoons (1 stick plus 2 tablespoons) unsalted butter, melted and cooled to room temperature, plus additional for greasing the pan

½ cup raspberry jam

2 large eggs, at room temperature

3 ounces bittersweet or semisweet chocolate, chopped, melted, and cooled to room temperature

2 ounces unsweetened chocolate, chopped, melted, and cooled to room temperature

2 teaspoons pure vanilla extract

1. Position the rack in the center of the oven; heat the oven to 350°F. Generously butter the inside of a 9-inch square pan.

2. Put the wheat berries in the large canister; cover and blend to a fine flour, about 1 minute. Add the sugar, baking soda, and salt; cover and pulse several times to combine. Pour the flour mixture into a large bowl.

3. Put the melted butter, jam, eggs, both types of melted chocolate, and the vanilla in the large canister. Cover and blend at low speed until smooth, about 10 seconds. Pour into the flour mixture and whisk until smooth. Pour and scrape the batter into the prepared pan.

4. Bake until puffed and set, until a toothpick or cake tester inserted into the center of the cake comes out with a few moist crumbs attached, 28 to 30 minutes. Cool in the pan on a wire rack for at least 1 hour before slicing into squares to serve. If desired, turn the brownie cake and its pan upside down onto a cutting board, remove the pan, and invert the brownie cake again, still on its cutting board, onto a serving platter or a second cutting board, all before slicing into squares.

NOTE: Substitute orange marmalade for the raspberry jam—the brownies will taste like orangettes!

CHOCOLATE CHIP BLONDIES

These are the classics: a moist cake with great crumb, laced with lots of chocolate chips. (And whole grain, too!) Cold milk and a cold egg will cause the butter to clump and the batter to stiffen. Make sure both are at room temperature. • MAKES 9 BLONDIES

1 cup soft white wheat berries

½ cup packed light brown sugar

¼ cup granulated white sugar

1 teaspoon baking powder

¼ teaspoon salt

8 tablespoons (1 stick) unsalted butter, melted and cooled to room temperature, plus additional for greasing the pan

⅓ cup whole milk, at room temperature

1 large egg, at room temperature

2 teaspoons pure vanilla extract

1 cup semisweet or bittersweet chocolate chips

2 tablespoons all-purpose flour

1. Position the rack in the center of the oven; heat the oven to 350°F. Generously butter the inside of an 8-inch square baking pan.

2. Put the wheat berries in the large canister; cover and blend at the highest speed to a fine flour, about 1 minute. Add the brown sugar, white sugar, baking powder, and salt; cover and pulse several times to combine. Pour the flour mixture into a large bowl.

3. Put the melted butter, milk, egg, and vanilla in the large canister. Cover and blend at low speed until smooth, about 10 seconds. Pour into the flour mixture and stir with a wooden spoon until smooth. Stir in the chocolate chips and all-purpose flour until well combined. Pour and scrape the batter into the prepared pan.

4. Bake until the top is set and very lightly browned, until a toothpick or cake tester inserted into the center of the cake, without touching a chocolate chip comes out clean, about 28 minutes. Cool in the pan on a wire rack for at least 1 hour before cutting into squares to serve.

COCONUT BLONDIES

Both coconut oil and shredded coconut make these blondies super moist but dense, even a little chewy. It's such a great flavor, you might need some ice cream to go along with a piece. Consider Banana Ice Cream (page 36) or Pineapple Ice Cream (page 37) for a tropical flourish. • MAKES 18 TO 24 BLONDIES

Unsalted butter, for greasing the pan

1½ cups soft white wheat berries

½ teaspoon baking powder

½ teaspoon baking soda

½ teaspoon salt

1 cup solid coconut oil, melted and cooled to room temperature (see Note)

1½ cups packed dark brown sugar

½ cup granulated white sugar

4 large eggs, at room temperature

2 teaspoons pure vanilla extract

1 cup semisweet or bittersweet chocolate chips

1 cup sweetened shredded coconut

1. Position the rack in the center of the oven; heat the oven to 350°F. Lightly and evenly butter the inside of a 9 x 13-inch baking dish.

2. Put the wheat berries in the large canister; cover and blend at the highest speed to a powdery flour, about 1 minute. Add the baking powder, baking soda, and salt; cover and pulse several times until evenly combined. Pour the flour mixture into a large bowl.

3. Put the coconut oil, brown sugar, white sugar, eggs, and vanilla in the large canister. Cover and blend at low speed until smooth, about 1 minute.

4. Pour the coconut mixture into the flour mixture and stir with a wooden spoon until evenly combined with no dry pockets of flour in the still somewhat grainy batter. Stir in the chocolate chips and coconut until evenly distributed. Pour and scrape the batter into the prepared pan.

5. Bake until the top of the cake is set and a toothpick or cake tester inserted into the center of the cake comes out clean, about 40 minutes. Cool in the pan on a wire rack for 1 hour before slicing into squares or rectangles to serve.

NOTE: Coconut oil is solid at room temperature. You'll need to scrape it out of its container with the tines of a fork. Pack it into the cup, then melt in a microwave-safe bowl by microwaving on high in 10-second bursts, stirring after each. Cool at room temperature for at least 20 minutes.

STRAWBERRY-RHUBARB CAKE

As this cake bakes, the strawberries and rhubarb begin to sink down into it, making it super moist, almost "pudding-cake-ish" in places. You might not get clean pieces out of the pan, but they'll be particularly welcome if they're still warm and you've got some vanilla ice cream or even sweetened vanilla yogurt on hand. · MAKES 6 TO 8 SERVINGS

1½ cups soft white wheat berries

1½ teaspoons baking powder

½ teaspoon salt

1½ cups granulated white sugar

3 large eggs, at room temperature

6 tablespoons (¾ stick) unsalted butter, melted and cooled to room temperature, plus additional for greasing the pan

¼ cup whole milk, at room temperature

2 teaspoons pure vanilla extract

2 cups sliced, hulled strawberries

2 cups sliced fresh rhubarb (see Note)

1. Position the rack in the center of the oven; heat the oven to 350°F. Lightly but evenly butter the inside of a 9-inch square baking pan.

2. Put the wheat berries in the large canister, cover and blend at the highest speed to a powder-like flour, about 1 minute. Add the baking powder and salt; pulse several times to combine evenly.

3. Add 1 cup of the sugar, the eggs, melted butter, milk, and vanilla. Cover and blend at low speed, repeatedly stopping the machine to scrape down the inside of the canister, or using the tamper, if available, until smooth, about 20 seconds. Pour and scrape the batter into the prepared pan.

4. Mix the strawberries, rhubarb, and the remaining ½ cup sugar in a medium bowl. Spread this mixture evenly over the top of the batter. Scrape the bowl well to get every drop!

5. Bake until set, puffed, and light brown, until a toothpick or cake tester inserted into the center of the cake comes out clean, about 45 minutes. Cool in the pan on a wire rack for at least 1 hour before slicing the cake into squares or rectangles to serve.

NOTE: To use frozen rhubarb, thaw 2¼ cups at room temperature, then pour off any liquid in the bowl and use only the drained rhubarb for the topping.

BLUEBERRY BUCKLE

This cake's a traditional "buckle," an American classic with the fruit mixed right into the batter (as opposed to the previous recipe with the berries on top). But don't worry: there's still a crumb topping—with coarsely ground wheat berries for even more crunch. Don't use frozen blueberries here. As they thaw, they'll make the batter soupy.

MAKES ABOUT 8 SERVINGS

FOR THE TOPPING

6 tablespoons soft white wheat berries

½ cup packed dark brown sugar

4 tablespoons (½ stick) unsalted butter, melted and cooled to room temperature, plus additional for greasing the pan

¼ teaspoon ground cinnamon

¼ teaspoon salt

⅛ teaspoon freshly grated nutmeg or a pinch of ground nutmeg

FOR THE CAKE

1 cup plus 2 tablespoons soft white wheat berries

⅔ cup granulated white sugar

1 teaspoon baking powder

½ teaspoon salt

8 tablespoons (1 stick) unsalted butter, melted and cooled to room temperature

½ cup whole milk, at room temperature

2 large eggs, at room temperature

2 teaspoons pure vanilla extract

2 cups fresh blueberries (about 7 ounces)

1. Position the rack in the center of the oven; heat the oven to 350°F. Lightly and evenly butter the inside of a 9-inch, high-sided, round baking pan, preferably a springform pan.

2. To make the topping, put the wheat berries in the large canister; cover and blend at the highest speed to a fine flour, about 30 seconds. Add the brown sugar, melted butter, cinnamon, salt, and nutmeg; cover and pulse until evenly combined. Pour the mixture into a medium bowl and set aside.

3. To make the cake, do not clean the canister. Put the wheat berries in the large canister; cover and blend at the highest speed until powdery and floury, about 1 minute. Add the granulated white sugar, baking powder, and salt; cover and blend at low speed until evenly combined, about 10 seconds. Add the melted butter, milk, eggs, and vanilla; cover and blend at low speed until smooth, about 30 seconds.

4. Remove the canister from the motor housing, add the blueberries, and gently stir in with a rubber spatula until evenly combined, taking care not to mash the blueberries too much. Pour and scrape the batter into the prepared pan. Crumble and sprinkle the topping mixture evenly on top.

5. Bake the buckle until the topping is lightly browned and a toothpick or cake tester inserted into the center of the cake comes out with a few moist crumbs attached, about 35 minutes, maybe a little longer depending on how wet the blueberries were. Cool in the pan on a wire rack for 1 hour before unlatching the sides of the springform pan, if using. Slice into wedges to serve.

PLUM CAKE

This cake is elegant enough for company. The pretty plum slices ring the top, keeping the (whole wheat!) cake underneath moist and tender. And since we're using oil and not butter, we don't have to worry about the ingredients being at room temperature—so things are even faster and easier here. Just remember the rule: there's not enough yogurt and sugar to cover up the taste of inferior, imitation vanilla. Use the best you can, usually labeled "pure vanilla extract"!

MAKES 8 SERVINGS

1½ cups soft white wheat berries

1 cup granulated white sugar

1 teaspoon baking powder

½ teaspoon baking soda

½ teaspoon ground cinnamon

¼ teaspoon salt

2 large eggs

½ cup plain, whole-milk yogurt

¼ cup vegetable or canola oil, plus additional for greasing the pan

1 teaspoon pure vanilla extract

3 large ripe plums, pitted and cut into thin slices

1. Position the rack in the center of the oven; heat the oven to 350°F. Lightly oil the inside of a 9-inch, high-sided, round baking pan, preferably a springform pan.

2. Put the wheat berries in the large canister; cover and blend at the highest speed to a fine flour, about 1 minute. Add the sugar, baking powder, baking soda, cinnamon, and salt; cover and pulse several times until evenly combined.

3. Add the eggs, yogurt, oil, and vanilla. Cover and blend at low speed, repeatedly stopping the machine to scrape down the inside of the canister, or using the tamper, if available, until smooth and thick, about 20 seconds. Pour and scrape the batter into the prepared pan. Top with the sliced plums.

4. Bake until the cake is set and a toothpick or cake tester inserted into the center comes out clean, about 40 minutes. Cool in the pan on a wire rack for at least 1 hour before unlatching the sides of the springform pan, if using. Slice into wedges to serve.

NOTE: You want enough sliced plums to cover the top of the cake. We actually called for a bit more than you need. We wanted to be safe rather than sorry.

RASPBERRY CRUMB CAKE

Here's a light cake baked under a fruit crisp! You make a whole grain batter, then add the berries and a light crumb topping—thus, a crisp baked over a cake. By lightly grinding the wheat berries for the topping, rather than grinding them to a fine flour, the crumb layer on top will retain a bit of crunch. • MAKES 6 TO 8 SERVINGS

FOR THE TOPPING

¼ cup soft white wheat berries

¼ cup granulated white sugar

3 tablespoons unsalted butter, melted and cooled to room temperature, plus additional for greasing the pan

¼ teaspoon ground cinnamon

⅛ teaspoon salt

FOR THE CAKE

1¾ cups soft white wheat berries

½ cup granulated white sugar

1 teaspoon baking powder

½ teaspoon salt

⅔ cup whole milk, at room temperature

8 tablespoons (1 stick) unsalted butter, melted and cooled to room temperature

2 large eggs, at room temperature

1 teaspoon pure vanilla extract

3 cups fresh raspberries (about 13 ounces—see Note)

1. Position the rack in the center of the oven; heat the oven to 350°F. Lightly and evenly butter the inside of a 9-inch baking pan.

2. To make the topping, put the wheat berries in the large canister; cover and blend at the highest speed until light and floury, about 30 seconds. Add the sugar, melted butter, cinnamon, and salt; cover and pulse until evenly combined—just a few pulses. Scrape the mixture into a medium bowl and set aside.

3. To make the cake, put the wheat berries in the large canister; cover and blend at the highest speed to a powdery flour, about 1 minute. Add the sugar, baking powder, and salt; cover and pulse until evenly combined. Add the milk, melted butter, eggs, and vanilla; cover and blend at low speed until smooth and thick, stopping the machine repeatedly to scrape down the inside of the canister, or using the tamper, if available, about 20 seconds.

4. Pour and scrape the batter into the prepared pan; top evenly with the fresh raspberries. Sprinkle and crumble the topping mixture evenly over the raspberries.

5. Bake until the cake is set and a toothpick or cake tester inserted into the center comes out clean, about 28 minutes. Cool in the pan on a wire rack for at least 30 minutes before slicing into 6 or 8 pieces to serve.

NOTE: If desired, substitute an equivalent weight (not volume) of blueberries or blackberries.

ALMOND BUTTER CAKE

This tasty cake is fairly simple: basically, you make a crunchy almond butter with the ground flour, then fold it into a fairly stiff batter. If you really want to go nuts, drizzle purchased raspberry ice cream topping over each serving. • MAKES 6 TO 8 SERVINGS

All-purpose flour, for dusting the baking pan

½ cup soft white wheat berries

1 cup sliced almonds

½ cup granulated white sugar

½ teaspoon baking powder

½ teaspoon salt

3 large eggs, at room temperature

8 tablespoons (1 stick) unsalted butter, melted and cooled to room temperature, plus additional for greasing the pan

1 tablespoon whole milk

2 teaspoons pure vanilla extract

Confectioners' sugar, for dusting

1. Position the rack in the center of the oven; heat the oven to 350°F. Lightly but evenly butter and then flour the inside of a 8-inch baking pan. Tap out any excess flour.

2. Put the wheat berries in the large canister; cover and blend at the highest speed to a fine flour, about 1 minute. Add the almonds; cover and blend at the highest speed until finely ground, even a little pasty, about 30 seconds.

3. Add the granulated white sugar, baking powder, and salt; pulse to combine. Add the eggs, melted butter, milk, and vanilla. Cover and blend at low speed, repeatedly stopping the machine to scrape down the inside of the canister, or using the tamper, if available, until smooth, about 20 seconds. Pour and scrape the batter into the prepared pan.

4. Bake until puffed and lightly browned, until a toothpick or cake tester inserted into the center of the cake comes out clean, about 35 minutes. Cool in the pan on a wire rack for at least 30 minutes before slicing into 6 rectangles to serve. If desired, dust each serving with confectioners' sugar.

NOTE: There's no worry about cold milk here because there's so little of it!

HONEY CAKE

There's only one secret to a honey cake: don't overbake it! The honey will begin to burn along the edges, giving the cake a slightly bitter flavor. Look for dark, dense, rich honeys at your supermarket or farmers' market, a treat far from the standard wildflower varietal. • MAKES 6 TO 8 SERVINGS

1½ cups soft white wheat berries

¼ cup packed light brown sugar

1 teaspoon baking soda

1 teaspoon ground cinnamon

¼ teaspoon ground allspice

¼ teaspoon salt

¾ cup honey

2 large eggs

⅓ cup whole milk

¼ cup canola or vegetable oil, plus additional for greasing the pan

1 tablespoon pure vanilla extract

1. Position the rack in the center of the oven; heat the oven to 300°F. Lightly but evenly oil the inside of a 9-inch, high-sided, round baking pan, preferably a springform pan.

2. Put the wheat berries in the large canister; cover and blend at the highest speed to a fine flour, about 1 minute. Add the sugar, baking soda, cinnamon, allspice, and salt; cover and pulse several times until evenly combined.

3. Add the honey, eggs, milk, oil, and vanilla. Cover and blend at low speed, stopping the machine repeatedly to scrape down the inside of the canister, or using the tamper, if available, until thick but uniform, about 20 seconds. Pour and scrape the batter into the prepared pan.

4. Bake until puffed and set, until a toothpick or cake tester inserted into the center of the cake comes out clean, 28 to 30 minutes. Cool in the pan on a wire rack for at least 30 minutes before slicing into squares or rectangles to serve.

GLUTEN-FREE LEMON BUTTERMILK CAKE

By working with a combination of grains, we can avoid chemical thickeners and stabilizers, the bane of gluten-free baking. We also get an amazing crumb by combining instant oats into the batter at the last moment. The resulting cake would welcome a scoop of vanilla ice cream on the side—or a generous dollop of whipped cream. • MAKES ABOUT 8 SERVINGS

½ cup yellow cornmeal

7 tablespoons buckwheat groats

3 tablespoons raw long-grain white rice

1 cup granulated white sugar

¼ cup cornstarch

1 teaspoon baking powder

1 teaspoon baking soda

½ teaspoon salt

⅔ cup regular buttermilk, at room temperature

8 tablespoons (1 stick) unsalted butter, melted and cooled to room temperature, plus additional for greasing the pan

2 large eggs, at room temperature

2 tablespoons fresh lemon juice

1 teaspoon lemon extract

½ cup certified gluten-free instant oats (see Note)

¾ cup raspberry jam

1. Position the rack in the center of the oven; heat the oven to 350°F. Generously butter the inside of a 9-inch round cake pan.

2. Put the cornmeal, buckwheat groats, and rice in the large canister; cover and blend at the highest speed to a fine flour, about 1 minute. Add the sugar, cornstarch, baking powder, baking soda, and salt; cover and blend at the highest speed for 10 seconds to combine. Add the buttermilk, melted butter, eggs, lemon juice, and lemon extract. Cover and blend at low speed until it is a fairly thin batter, about like a pancake batter that's just slightly thickened, about 20 seconds. Add the oats, cover, and blend at low speed for 5 seconds to combine. Pour the batter into the prepared pan.

3. Bake until firm and set, until a toothpick or cake tester inserted into the center of the cake comes out clean, about 30 minutes. Cool in the pan on a wire rack for 10 minutes, then turn the cake out, remove the pan, invert the cake onto a cutting board, and continue to cool to room temperature, about 1 ½ hours.

4. Just before serving, spread the jam over the top of the cake—or cut the cake into wedges and spoon the jam over and across each individual serving.

NOTE: Make sure those oats are instant oats (not old-fashioned rolled or steel-cut).

MARBLE BUNDT CAKE

We love Bundt cakes! They're like the best coffee cakes combined with the more sophisticated texture of a buttery layer cake. There's quite a bit of batter here so you'll really need to work with it to get it smooth and consistent in the canister before it goes into the pan. Who's put up a pot of coffee?

MAKES 10 TO 12 SERVINGS

1¾ cups soft white wheat berries

1½ teaspoons baking powder

¼ teaspoon salt

1 cup granulated white sugar

11 tablespoons (1 stick plus 3 tablespoons) unsalted butter, melted and cooled to room temperature, plus additional for greasing the pan

1 cup whole milk, at room temperature

2 large eggs, at room temperature

1 tablespoon pure vanilla extract

1 ounce unsweetened chocolate, melted and cooled to room temperature

1. Position the rack in the center of the oven; heat the oven to 350°F. Lightly but evenly butter the inside of a 10-inch round Bundt pan.

2. Put the wheat berries in the large canister; cover and blend at the highest speed to a fine flour, about 1 minute. Add the baking powder and salt and pulse a few times until evenly combined.

3. Add the sugar, melted butter, milk, eggs, and vanilla. Cover and blend at medium speed, stopping the machine occasionally to scrape down the insides of the canister, or using the tamper, if available, until uniform and smooth, about 30 seconds.

4. Pour and scrape about half the batter in the canister into a large bowl. Stir in the melted chocolate until smooth. Alternately pour and scrape the batters into the prepared pan, creating a marbled appearance.

5. Bake until lightly browned and a toothpick or cake tester inserted into the center of the cake comes out clean, 28 to 30 minutes. Cool in the pan on a wire rack for 10 minutes, then invert the cake and pan onto a serving platter and remove the pan. Cool the cake for at least another 30 minutes before slicing into wedges to serve.

APPLE BUTTER BUNDT CAKE WITH A MAPLE GLAZE

If it's autumn in your neck of the woods, you'll want to make this simple Bundt cake when you've got friends or family stopping by. It's terrific with a cup of tea. If you want to spice it up a bit, add 1 teaspoon ground cinnamon and ½ teaspoon ground allspice with the milk. • MAKES 10 TO 12 SERVINGS

FOR THE CAKE

All-purpose flour, for dusting the pan

1¼ cups soft white wheat berries

1 teaspoon baking powder

½ teaspoon baking soda

¼ teaspoon salt

1 cup apple butter (see Note)

¾ cup granulated white sugar

8 tablespoons (1 stick) unsalted butter, melted and cooled to room temperature, plus additional for greasing the pan

2 large eggs, at room temperature

¼ cup whole milk, at room temperature

FOR THE GLAZE

¼ cup maple syrup, preferably Grade B or 2

2 tablespoons unsalted butter, melted and cooled to room temperature

1 to 2 cups confectioners' sugar

1. Position the rack in the center of the oven; heat the oven to 350°F. Lightly but evenly butter and flour the inside of a 10-inch round Bundt cake. Tap out any excess flour.

2. Put the wheat berries in the large canister; cover and blend to a fine flour, about 1 minute. Add the baking powder, baking soda, and salt; cover and blend at the highest speed until well combined, about 10 seconds.

3. Add the apple butter, granulated white sugar, melted butter, eggs, and milk. Cover and blend at medium speed, repeatedly stopping the machine to scrape down the inside of the canister, or using the tamper, if available, until uniform and thick, about 30 seconds. Pour and scrape the batter into the prepared pan.

4. Bake until puffed and set, until a toothpick or cake tester inserted into the center of the cake comes out clean, about 35 minutes. Cool in the pan on a wire rack for 10 minutes, then invert the cake and pan onto a serving platter and remove the pan. Cool to room temperature, about 1½ hours.

5. To make the glaze, whisk the maple syrup and melted butter in a large bowl. Add 1 cup of the confectioners' sugar and whisk until smooth. Continue adding more confectioners' sugar in 2-tablespoon increments until you achieve a thickened but "drizzle-able" glaze. Drizzle over the cake off the tines of a fork, then set the cake aside for at least 10 minutes, or up to 1 hour before slicing into wedges to serve.

NOTE: Feel free to substitute pumpkin butter for the apple butter.

PINEAPPLE UPSIDE-DOWN CAKE

Break out the Buddy Holly records! Here's a retro dessert that's always welcome. We add coconut to keep the cake extra-moist in the presence of those healthy whole grains. If you want, set halved, stemmed maraschino cherries in the spaces between the pineapple chunks before adding the batter.

MAKES ABOUT 8 SERVINGS

11 tablespoons (1 stick plus 3 tablespoons) unsalted butter, melted and cooled

6 tablespoons packed dark brown sugar

One 20-ounce can pineapple chunks in heavy syrup, drained

¾ cup plus 2 tablespoons soft white wheat berries

¾ cup granulated white sugar

½ teaspoon baking powder

½ teaspoon salt

3 large eggs, plus 1 large egg yolk, at room temperature

1 teaspoon pure vanilla extract

1 cup shredded sweetened coconut

1. Position the rack in the middle of the oven; heat the oven to 350°F. Lightly butter the inside of an 8-inch round cake pan.

2. Mix 3 tablespoons of the melted butter and the brown sugar in a small bowl, then spread this mixture evenly into the cake pan. Cover this mixture with the pineapple pieces.

3. Put the wheat berries in the large canister; cover and blend at the highest speed to a fine flour, about 1 minute. Add the granulated white sugar, baking powder, and salt; cover and pulse several times until well combined. Add the eggs, egg yolk, vanilla, and the remaining 8 tablespoons melted butter. Cover and blend at low speed, repeatedly stopping the machine to scrape down the inside of the canister, or using the tamper, if available, about 20 seconds.

4. Remove the canister from the power housing, add the coconut to the canister, and use a rubber spatula to fold it into the batter. Carefully pour, scrape, and spread the batter over the pineapple in the prepared pan.

5. Bake until puffed and lightly browned, until a toothpick or cake tester inserted into the center of the cake without touching the pineapple below comes out clean, about 40 minutes. Cool the cake on a wire rack for 5 minutes, then set a serving platter over the pan and invert the whole thing onto the platter. Remove the still warm cake pan, allowing the syrup to run down the sides of the cake. Cool for at least another 30 minutes before slicing into wedges to serve.

NOTE: Butter the pan well to keep the cake from sticking. If some of the pineapple stays behind, or gets jostled a bit when unmolding, set it back in place with a rubber spatula.

PEACH UPSIDE-DOWN CAKE

Make sure the peaches are ripe but not mushy. They should smell sweet and delectable. There's not as much batter here as there is with some of the other cakes. We wanted a relatively thin layer that didn't overwhelm the peaches. Scrape out almost every drop, gently dolloping and smoothing it to create an even layer over the peaches without pressing down on them. • MAKES ABOUT 10 SERVINGS

4 ripe, sweet peaches, peeled and thinly sliced

3 tablespoons packed light brown sugar

½ cup soft white wheat berries

½ cup granulated white sugar

¼ cup yellow cornmeal

½ teaspoon baking powder

½ teaspoon ground cinnamon

½ teaspoon salt

8 tablespoons (1 stick) unsalted butter, melted and cooled, plus additional for greasing the pan

2 large eggs, at room temperature

2 tablespoons whole milk

½ teaspoon almond extract

1. Position the rack in the center of the oven; heat the oven to 350°F. Heavily butter the inside of a 9-inch round cake pan. Place the peach slices in a decorative pattern in the bottom of the prepared cake pan. Sprinkle the brown sugar evenly over them.

2. Put the wheat berries in the large canister; cover and blend at the highest speed to a fine flour, about 1 minute. Add the granulated white sugar, cornmeal, baking powder, cinnamon, and salt; cover and blend at low speed to combine, about 10 seconds.

3. Add the melted butter, eggs, milk, and almond extract. Cover and blend at low speed, stopping the machine repeatedly to scrape down the inside of the canister, or using the tamper, if available, until smooth, about 20 seconds. Pour and spread the batter over the peaches in the pan.

4. Bake until puffed and set, until a toothpick or cake tester inserted into the center of the cake without touching a peach comes out with a few moist crumbs attached, about 30 minutes. Cool the cake in the pan on a wire rack for 5 minutes, then set a serving platter over the pan and invert the whole thing onto the platter. Remove the pan and nudge any dislodged peach slices back in place with a rubber spatula. Cool for at least another 30 minutes before slicing into wedges to serve.

BANANA UPSIDE-DOWN CAKE

One more upside-down cake! (Can there be too many?) This one's sort of like a cross between a banana bread and a traditional cake. Maybe you'd want to serve it for brunch this weekend? • MAKES ABOUT 10 SERVINGS

10 tablespoons (1 stick plus 2 tablespoons) unsalted butter, melted and cooled, plus additional for greasing the pan

½ cup packed dark brown sugar

2 medium ripe bananas, peeled and sliced, plus 1 small banana, peeled

¾ cup plus 2 tablespoons soft white wheat berries

½ cup granulated white sugar

2 teaspoons baking powder

½ teaspoon ground cinnamon

½ teaspoon salt

1 large egg, at room temperature

½ cup whole milk, at room temperature

1. Position the rack in the center of the oven; heat the oven to 350°F. Generously butter the inside of a 9-inch round cake pan.

2. Mix 6 tablespoons of the melted butter and the brown sugar in a small bowl; spread evenly across the bottom of the prepared pan. Lay the sliced medium bananas on top of the sugar mixture.

3. Put the wheat berries in the large canister; cover and blend at the highest speed to a fine flour, about 1 minute. Add the granulated white sugar, baking powder, cinnamon, and salt; cover and pulse several times to combine.

4. Pour in the remaining melted butter; add the remaining small banana, egg, and milk. Cover and blend at low speed, repeatedly stopping the machine to scrape down the inside of the canister, or using the tamper, if available, until uniform and thick, about 20 seconds. Pour and spread this batter over the bananas in the prepared pan.

5. Bake until puffed and set, until a toothpick or cake tester inserted into the center of the cake without touching a banana slice comes out with a few moist crumbs attached, about 30 minutes. Cool the cake in the pan on a wire rack for 5 minutes, then set a serving platter over the pan and invert the whole thing onto the platter. Remove the pan, nudge any dislodged bananas into place with a rubber spatula, and continue cooling for at least 30 minutes before slicing into wedges to serve.

CHOCOLATE LAYER CAKE WITH OLD-FASHIONED SEVEN-MINUTE FROSTING

This layer cake is exceptionally light, especially for whole grain baking. We wanted its texture to match the "marshmallowy" frosting, something of a Southern tradition. You'll need to watch carefully as you make the frosting—it's done in exactly seven minutes at sea level (or a little less at higher altitudes). You'll also make a lot. We wanted enough so you could frost the cake with ease. If you want to use up the remainder, dip salty pretzel sticks in it for a crazy treat. • MAKES 10 TO 12 SERVINGS

FOR THE CAKE

6 tablespoons (¾ stick) unsalted butter, plus additional for greasing the pans

3 ounces unsweetened chocolate, chopped

1½ cups soft white wheat berries

1½ cups granulated white sugar

2 tablespoons unsweetened cocoa powder

1 teaspoon baking powder

½ teaspoon baking soda

½ teaspoon salt

1 cup whole milk, at room temperature

2 large eggs, plus 1 large egg yolk, at room temperature

1 teaspoon pure vanilla extract

FOR THE FROSTING

3 large egg whites

2¼ cups granulated white sugar

½ cup water

2 teaspoons light corn syrup

2 teaspoons pure vanilla extract

½ teaspoon salt

1. To make the cake, position the rack in the center of the oven; heat the oven to 325°F. Generously butter the inside of two 8-inch round cake pans.

2. Put the butter and chocolate in a small microwave-safe bowl. Microwave on high in 10-second increments, stirring after each, until all the butter and most of the chocolate has melted. Stir at room temperature until all the chocolate has melted. Cool for 15 minutes.

3. Put the wheat berries in the large canister; cover and blend at the highest speed to a fine flour, about 1 minute. Add the sugar, cocoa, baking powder, baking soda, and salt; cover and blend at low speed until uniform, about 10 seconds.

4. Add the butter-chocolate mixture along with the milk, eggs, egg yolk, and vanilla. Cover and blend at low speed, stopping the machine repeatedly to scrape down the inside of the canister, or using the tamper, if available, until smooth, about 20 seconds. Divide and spread the batter equally into the prepared pans.

5. Bake until puffed and set, until a toothpick or cake tester inserted into the center of each cake comes out clean, about 20 minutes. Cool the cakes in the pans on a wire rack for 15 minutes, then invert onto the rack, remove the pans, and continue cooling to room temperature, at least 1 hour.

6. To make the frosting, bring about 1 inch of water to a boil in the bottom half of a double boiler set over high heat. Reduce the heat to very low so that the water bubbles slowly. Pour the egg whites, sugar, water, corn syrup, vanilla, and salt in the top half of the double boiler; set it over the simmering water; and, using an electric mixer at medium speed, beat until creamy and light, about like Marshmallow Fluff, exactly 7 minutes at sea level, a little less at high elevations.

7. To frost the cake, follow the directions in step 6 of the recipe for Vanilla Layer Cake with Lemon Buttercream on page 118.

VANILLA SHEET CAKE WITH CHOCOLATE FROSTING

If you grew up in the South, you know about sheet cakes. They're baked in large, rimmed baking sheets: 11 x 17 inches, the American standard. You end up with a giant, thin cake that you can slather with lots of frosting. In fact, you never have to worry about portioning out the cake-to-frosting ratio ever again!

MAKES 26 TO 30 SERVINGS

FOR THE CAKE

All-purpose flour, for dusting the pan

1¾ cups soft white wheat berries

1½ teaspoons baking soda

1 teaspoon salt

½ teaspoon ground cinnamon

1¾ cups granulated white sugar

1½ cups regular buttermilk, at room temperature

16 tablespoons (2 sticks) unsalted butter, melted and cooled to room temperature, plus additional for greasing the pan

2 large eggs, at room temperature

1 tablespoon pure vanilla extract

FOR THE FROSTING

12 tablespoons (1½ sticks) unsalted butter, melted and cooled to room temperature

3 tablespoons unsweetened cocoa powder

3 tablespoons whole milk

2 teaspoon pure vanilla extract

5 cups confectioners' sugar

1. To make the sheet cake, position the rack in the center of the oven; heat the oven to 375°F. Lightly but evenly butter the inside of an 11 x 17-inch rimmed baking sheet (see Note). Dust the buttered pan with flour, coating it evenly before tapping out any excess.

2. Put the wheat berries in the large canister; cover and blend at the highest speed to a fine flour, about 1 minute. Add the baking soda, salt, and cinnamon; cover and pulse several times until combined.

3. Add the granulated white sugar, buttermilk, melted butter, eggs, and vanilla. Cover and blend at low speed until smooth, repeatedly stopping the machine to scrape down the inside of the canister, or using the tamper, if available, until thick and smooth, about 20 seconds. Pour, scrape, and even out the batter in the prepared pan.

4. Bake until puffed, set to the touch, very lightly browned, and a toothpick or cake tester inserted into the center of the cake comes out clean, 15 to 17 minutes. Cool the cake in the pan on a wire rack to room temperature, at least 1 hour.

5. To make the frosting, whisk the melted butter, cocoa powder, milk, and vanilla in a large bowl until smooth. Add about half the confectioners' sugar and whisk until smooth. Gradually add more and more confectioners' sugar until thick but spreadable. Spread and smooth the glaze over the cake; set aside for at least 15 minutes to let the glaze set up. Cut the cake into squares or rectangles to serve.

NOTE: The baking sheet *must not* be insulated for the batter to set properly.

VANILLA LAYER CAKE WITH LEMON BUTTERCREAM

We've paired this light cake with a lemony buttercream, the perfect match for any celebration. • MAKES ABOUT 12 SERVINGS

FOR THE CAKE

All-purpose flour, for dusting the pan

1½ cups soft white wheat berries

1 teaspoon baking powder

¼ teaspoon baking soda

¼ teaspoon salt

12 tablespoons (1½ sticks) unsalted butter, melted and cooled to room temperature, plus additional for greasing the pans

1 cup granulated white sugar

4 large eggs, at room temperature

½ cup whole milk, at room temperature

1 tablespoon pure vanilla extract

FOR THE BUTTERCREAM

16 tablespoons (2 sticks) unsalted butter, at room temperature

3 to 4 cups confectioners' sugar (see Note)

¼ cup heavy cream, at room temperature

3 tablespoons lemon juice

1 teaspoon pure vanilla extract

¼ teaspoon salt

1. Position the rack in the center of the oven; heat the oven to 350°F. Lightly but evenly butter the inside of two 8-inch round cake pans. Dust both with flour, coating evenly, then tap out the excess.

2. Put the wheat berries in the large canister; cover and blend at the highest speed to a fine flour, about 1 minute. Add the baking powder, baking soda, and salt; cover and pulse to combine.

3. Add the melted butter, granulated white sugar, eggs, milk, and vanilla. Cover and blend at low speed, repeatedly stopping the machine to scrape down the inside of the canister, or using the tamper, if available, until smooth, about 20 seconds. Divide the batter equally between the two prepared pans, smoothing it to an even depth.

4. Bake until lightly browned and set to the touch, until a toothpick or cake tester inserted into the center of both cakes comes out clean, 18 to 20 minutes. Cool the cakes in the pans on a wire rack for 10 minutes, then invert and remove the pans. Invert the cakes again, top side up, and continue to cool to room temperature, at least 1 hour.

5. To make the buttercream, put the butter in a large bowl, add the confectioners' sugar in 1-cup increments, and beat with an electric mixer at medium speed until smooth. Beat in the cream, then beat in the lemon juice, vanilla, and salt.

6. To frost the cake, set one layer top side down on a cake stand and spread about 1 cup of the frosting over the top of the layer. Set the second layer top side up on the first layer. Spoon most of the frosting into the center of the top of the cake and spread it to the edges, letting it slide over the edge and spreading it around the sides as well. Slice the cake into wedges to serve.

NOTE: 3½ cups of confectioners' sugar is about what you'll get out of a 1-pound bag.

DEVIL'S FOOD SHEET CAKE WITH CREAM CHEESE FROSTING

"Devil's Food" originally indicated a chocolate angel food cake. Get it? It's "angel food" turned dark. But these days, it means any rich chocolate cake. We've packed this one with lots of cocoa powder to give it great flavor and texture. • MAKES 16 TO 20 SERVINGS

FOR THE CAKE

All-purpose flour, for dusting the baking pan

1¾ cups soft white wheat berries

⅔ cup unsweetened cocoa powder

1 teaspoon baking soda

½ teaspoon salt

1½ cups whole milk, at room temperature

1 cup granulated white sugar

¾ cup packed dark brown sugar

12 tablespoons (1½ sticks) unsalted butter, melted and cooled to room temperature, plus additional for greasing the pan

3 large eggs, at room temperature

2 teaspoons pure vanilla extract

FOR THE FROSTING

8 tablespoons (1 stick) unsalted butter, at room temperature

8 ounces regular or low-fat cream cheese, at room temperature

½ cup packed light brown sugar

½ cup regular or low-fat sour cream, at room temperature

2 teaspoons pure vanilla extract

5½ to 7 cups confectioners' sugar

1. To make the cake, position the rack in the center of the oven; heat the oven to 350°F. Lightly but evenly butter the inside of an 11 x 17-inch rimmed baking sheet. Dust it with flour and coat evenly, tapping out any excess.

2. Put the wheat berries in the large canister; cover and blend at the highest speed to a fine flour, about 1 minute. Add the cocoa powder, baking soda, and salt; cover and pulse several times to combine.

3. Add the milk, granulated white sugar, dark brown sugar, melted butter, eggs, and vanilla. Cover and blend at low speed, repeatedly stopping the machine to scrape down the inside of the canister, or using the tamper, if available, until uniform and thick, about 20 seconds. Pour, scrape, and even out the batter in the prepared pan.

4. Bake until puffed and set, until a toothpick or a cake tester inserted into the center of the cake comes out clean, 15 to 17 minutes. Cool the cake in the pan on a wire rack to room temperature, at least 1 hour.

5. To make the frosting, put the butter and cream cheese in a large bowl and beat with an electric mixer at medium speed until soft and smooth, scraping down the inside of the bowl occasionally. Add the light brown sugar, sour cream, and vanilla; continue beating until smooth. Scrape down the bowl and remove the beaters. Stir in 4 cups of the confectioners' sugar with a rubber spatula until smooth, then add more confectioners' sugar, at first in ⅓-cup increments and then less and less, until smooth and spreadable. Spread the frosting evenly over the cooled cake, then slice into squares and rectangles to serve.

CRISPS, COBBLERS, & OTHER FRUIT DESSERTS

THERE ARE CAKE PEOPLE AND THERE ARE PIE PEOPLE. WE SATISFIED THE FIRST GROUP WITH THE FIRST PART OF THIS CHAPTER. NOW TO TURN THOSE OF US WHO LOVE FRESH FRUIT FILLINGS IN ALL THEIR INCARNATIONS.

No, we can't pull an apple pie out of a turbo blender. But as you'll see, we can make a pretty fine apple crisp.

Most of these fruit dessert recipes simplify our use of the blender: we make the topping—crumb, crisp, or cobbler—in the blender, then sprinkle it over a fruit mixture in the pan. Our real purpose for the blender is to create a whole grain topping over fruit, easy and wholesome.

There are a few desserts in this section that are a tad out of that norm. We've got a clafouti, an old French classic—and a one-canister wonder from the blender. Basically, it's a thickened egg custard poured over fresh fruit and then baked. It's fresh, summery fare, best on a sunny weekend.

And we've got two American classics that may have been forgotten by most of us (or never known): cranberry pie, something of a tradition in our New England part the woods; and sonker, a North Carolina specialty that's like a rich cobbler with fruit baked under a buttery batter.

NUTS

Out of their shells, they go rancid quickly—and ruin a crisp without hesitation. Store shelled nuts in the refrigerator in sealed containers for a couple of weeks. Or store them in the freezer for several months. There's no need to thaw them before you use them in any of these recipes.

INSTANT TAPIOCA

It's an old-fashioned baking standard: basically ground bits of tapioca starch. It lets us cut down on the flour in the fillings, thereby rendering them less gummy and more luxurious. You'll find it in the baking aisle of almost all North American supermarkets. Store an opened container in a sealed plastic bag (to prevent spills) in a dark pantry for up to 1 year.

SO LET'S GET to making fresh fruit desserts. Remember the rule: use the freshest fruit you can find. These concoctions are worth it.

APPLE-PECAN CRISP

Here's a classic made better: we can offer a bit more body to the topping with a whole grain flour from the turbo blender, then grind the nuts a little more finely for a smoother, richer finish. Who's got the vanilla ice cream? MAKES 6 TO 8 SERVINGS

2½ pounds firm, tart apples, such as Granny Smith apples, peeled, cored, and thinly sliced

⅓ cup plus 6 tablespoons granulated white sugar

⅓ cup packed dark brown sugar

1½ tablespoons all-purpose flour

1 tablespoon instant tapioca

1 teaspoon fresh lemon juice

1 teaspoon ground cinnamon

½ teaspoon salt

1 cup soft white wheat berries

½ cup pecan or walnut pieces

6 tablespoons (¾ stick) unsalted butter, melted and cooled

1. Position the rack in the center of the oven; heat the oven to 350°F.

2. Mix the apples, ⅓ cup of the granulated white sugar, the brown sugar, flour, instant tapioca, lemon juice, ½ teaspoon of the cinnamon, and ¼ teaspoon of the salt in a large bowl. Pour into a 9-inch square baking pan, scraping in every last drop. Do not wash the bowl; set it aside.

3. Put the wheat berries in the large canister; cover and blend at the highest speed to a very coarse flour, not a fine flour at all, about 25 seconds. Add the nuts, the remaining 6 tablespoons white sugar, the remaining ½ teaspoon cinnamon, and the remaining

¼ teaspoon salt. Pulse several times to grind the nuts a bit. Pour the mixture into the reserved large bowl. Stir in the melted butter until evenly moistened. Crumble this mixture over the apple mixture in the pan.

4. Bake the crisp until the topping has browned and the filling is bubbling, about 40 minutes. Cool in the pan on a wire rack for at least 15 minutes before serving.

PEACH CRISP WITH AN OAT-ALMOND TOPPING

You'll need ripe peaches to make a successful filling that stands up to this crunchy, granola-like topping. Instead of vanilla ice cream on top, how about cherry vanilla? Or even raspberry sherbet? • MAKES 6 TO 8 SERVINGS

2½ pounds ripe peaches, peeled, pitted, and thinly sliced (about 6 cups)

⅔ cup granulated white sugar

2½ tablespoons instant tapioca

½ teaspoon pure vanilla extract

¼ teaspoon almond extract

¾ cup soft white wheat berries

¾ cup old-fashioned rolled oats (do not use quick-cooking or steel-cut oats)

½ cup packed light brown sugar

½ cup sliced almonds

½ teaspoon ground cinnamon

½ teaspoon salt

6 tablespoons (¾ stick) unsalted butter, melted and cooled to room temperature, plus additional for greasing the pan

6 tablespoons maple syrup, preferably Grade B or 2

1. Position the rack in the center of the oven; heat the oven to 350°F. Lightly but evenly butter the inside of a 9-inch square baking dish.

2. Mix the peaches, granulated white sugar, tapioca, vanilla, and almond extracts in a large bowl. Pour into the prepared baking dish, scraping in every last drop from the bowl. Do not wash this bowl; set it aside.

3. Put the wheat berries in the large canister; cover and blend at the highest speed to a coarse flour, about 25 seconds. Add the oats, brown sugar, almonds, cinnamon, and salt; cover and pulse 2 or 3 times to roughly chop the oats and nuts. Pour this mixture into the reserved bowl. Stir in the melted butter and maple syrup to form a loose crumble. Sprinkle the crumble evenly over the top of the peach mixture.

4. Bake the crisp until the topping has lightly browned and the peach mixture is bubbling below, about 45 minutes. Cool in the pan on a wire rack for at least 15 minutes before serving.

PEAR CRISP WITH A GINGER-WALNUT TOPPING

Here's one last crisp, this one with an even more flavorful topping to match up with those luscious pears. In truth, you could mix and match any of the toppings for these crisps— for example, by putting this ginger-walnut fandango over the peach filling in the last recipe. · MAKES 6 TO 8 SERVINGS

3 pounds ripe pears, peeled, cored, and thinly sliced

½ cup granulated white sugar

2 tablespoons honey

2 tablespoons instant tapioca

1 tablespoon fresh lemon juice

¼ teaspoon ground dried ginger

¼ teaspoon freshly grated nutmeg or ⅛ teaspoon ground nutmeg

1 cup plus 2 tablespoons soft white wheat berries

½ cup walnut pieces

¼ cup chopped candied ginger (a.k.a. crystallized ginger)

6 tablespoons (¾ stick) unsalted butter, melted and cooled to room temperature

1. Position the rack in the center of the oven; heat the oven to 350°F.

2. Mix the pears, ¼ cup of the sugar, the honey, instant tapioca, lemon juice, ground ginger, and nutmeg in a large bowl. Pour into a 9-inch square baking pan, making sure you get every drop from the bowl. Do not wash this bowl; set it aside.

3. Put the wheat berries in the large canister; cover and blend at the highest speed to a

very coarse flour, about 30 seconds. Add the walnuts, candied ginger, and the remaining ¼ cup sugar. Cover and pulse 2 or 3 times to chop the nuts a bit finer. Pour into the reserved bowl. Stir in the melted butter until evenly and well moistened. Crumble this mixture evenly over the pear mixture in the pan.

4. Bake the crisp until the topping has browned and the filling is bubbling below, about 40 minutes. Cool in the pan on a wire rack for at least 15 minutes before serving.

PLUM COBBLER

There are no eggs in the batter to top this cobbler. The resulting mixture will be much looser than a standard biscuit topping; it will not mound on a spoon or in the pan but instead makes a flatter topping that submerges into the fruit below, like all the bread and jam mixed together that anyone could want.

MAKES 6 SERVINGS

5 cups sliced, pitted plums
(6 to 8 medium plums)

1 cup granulated white sugar

1½ tablespoons instant tapioca

½ teaspoon salt

1 cup soft white wheat berries

1 teaspoon baking powder

½ teaspoon ground cinnamon

¼ teaspoon salt

½ cup whole or 2 percent milk, at room temperature

3 tablespoons unsalted butter, melted and cooled to room temperature, plus additional for greasing the pan

1. Position the rack in the center of the oven; heat the oven to 350°F. Lightly but evenly butter the inside of an 8-inch baking pan.

2. Mix the plums, ¾ cup of the sugar, the tapioca, and salt in a large bowl. Pour into the prepared pan.

3. Put the wheat berries in the large canister; cover and blend at the highest speed to a fine flour, about 1 minute. Add the remaining ¼ cup sugar, the baking powder, ground cinnamon, and salt. Cover and blend at low speed to combine, about 10 seconds.

4. Add the milk and melted butter. Cover and blend at low speed to create a thick batter, stopping the machine the minute it begins to strain. Using a flatware tablespoon, dollop the batter evenly over the plum mixture.

5. Bake the cobbler until the topping is lightly browned and the filling below is bubbling, 35 to 40 minutes. Cool in the pan on a wire rack for at least 15 minutes before serving.

NOTE: Throughout this section, you can just about mix and match any crisp cobbler topping over any fruit filling.

BLUEBERRY COBBLER
WITH TURBO BLENDER CRÈME ANGLAISE

For this cobbler, we mix the fruit filling together, then create a whole-grain biscuit topping in the blender canister. The only problem is that the biscuit-like topping gets pretty thick (but we can then create nice, rounded mounds over the fruit). You'll need to stop the blender a lot or use the tamper to get it blended smoothly without straining the motor. But the results will be worth the effort—particularly when you pair it with this easy version of a classic, French, vanilla custard sauce. • MAKES ABOUT 6 SERVINGS

5 cups fresh blueberries

⅓ cup plus 3 tablespoons granulated white sugar

2 tablespoons instant tapioca

1 tablespoon fresh lemon juice

½ teaspoon salt

1 cup soft white wheat berries

1½ teaspoons baking powder

3 tablespoons unsalted butter, melted and cooled to room temperature

3 tablespoons regular buttermilk

1 large egg, plus 1 large egg yolk, at room temperature

1 teaspoon pure vanilla extract

1. To make the cobbler, position the rack in the center of the oven; heat the oven to 350°F.

2. Mix the blueberries, ⅓ cup of the sugar, the tapioca, lemon juice, and ¼ teaspoon of the salt in a large bowl. Pour into an 8-inch square pan, scraping out every drop.

3. Put the wheat berries in the large canister; cover and blend at the highest speed to a fine flour, about 1 minute. Add the baking powder, the remaining 3 tablespoons sugar, and the remaining ¼ teaspoon salt. Cover and blend, pulsing several times to combine.

4. Add the melted butter, buttermilk, egg, egg yolk, and vanilla. Cover and blend at low speed, repeatedly stopping the blender to scrape down the inside of the canister, or using the tamper, if available, until smooth and very thick, like thick cornbread batter, about 20 seconds. Using a flatware tablespoon, dollop the batter all over the blueberry mixture.

5. Bake the cobbler until the topping has browned and the filling below is bubbling, 30 to 35 minutes. Cool on a wire rack for at least 30 minutes or to room temperature before serving.

TURBO BLENDER CRÈME ANGLAISE

Crème anglaise (*crehm AHN-glaiz*) is French for "English cream" and refers to a delicate custard sauce, usually made by stirring and stirring the mixture over very low heat until slightly thickened, so that it's about like room temperature, melted premium vanilla ice cream. But a high-powdered blender makes it so easy that you'll soon be pouring crème anglaise over every dessert! (Try it over chocolate cake or gingerbread and you'll see why we're so excited about it.) • MAKES ABOUT 2 CUPS

(continued)

1½ cups whole or 2 percent milk

½ cup granulated white sugar

¼ cup heavy cream

4 large egg yolks, at room temperature

2 teaspoons pure vanilla extract

2 teaspoons cornstarch

1. Pour the milk, sugar, cream, egg yolks, and vanilla into a cleaned and dry large canister. Cover and blend at the highest speed until steaming (about 120°F), approximately 4 minutes.

2. Add the cornstarch, cover, and blend at the highest speed until somewhat thickened, about like a milk shake, and until the temperature reaches 170°F, 1 to 2 minutes more. Pour the sauce into a large container and refrigerate for at least 3 hours, or up to 3 days, covering with plastic wrap once chilled.

RASPBERRY COBBLER WITH A BROWN SUGAR CAKE TOPPING

This topping is sort of like a quick bread baked on top of the fruit. Notice that the eggs and milk must be at room temperature. And you must use fresh raspberries for a successful set in the filling. • MAKES 6 TO 8 SERVINGS

6 cups fresh raspberries (about 1½ pounds)

½ cup granulated white sugar

2 tablespoons instant tapioca

½ teaspoon salt

¾ cup plus 2 tablespoons soft white wheat berries

¼ cup packed dark brown sugar

1½ teaspoons baking powder

⅓ cup whole or 2 percent milk, at room temperature

1 large egg, plus 1 large egg yolk, at room temperature

3 tablespoons unsalted butter, melted and cooled to room temperature

1 teaspoon pure vanilla extract

1. Position the rack in the center of the oven; heat the oven to 350°F.

2. Mix the raspberries, granulated white sugar, tapioca, and ¼ teaspoon salt in a large bowl. Pour into a 9-inch square baking pan.

3. Put the wheat berries in the large canister; cover and blend at the highest speed to a fine flour, about 1 minute. Add the brown sugar, baking powder, and the remaining ¼ teaspoon salt. Cover and blend at low speed until combined, about 10 seconds.

4. Add the milk, egg, egg yolk, melted butter, and vanilla. Cover and blend at low speed, repeatedly stopping the machine to scrape down the inside of the canister, or using the tamper, if available, until smooth but a little thinner than a standard dough, about 10 seconds. Spoon the batter evenly over the raspberry mixture.

5. Bake the cobbler until the top has lightly browned and the fruit filling is bubbling, about 45 minutes. Cool in the pan on a wire rack for at least 15 minutes, or to room temperature, before serving.

NEW ENGLAND CRANBERRY PIE

Here's a blast from the past, sometimes called Nantucket or Cape Cod Pie. It's a tart-sweet mix fit for a fall evening. The custard-like filling sets into a chewy, meringue-like, crackled crust over the cranberries. You'll be able to cut slices like any other pie, the berries on the bottom. • MAKES ABOUT 8 SERVINGS

2 cups fresh or frozen cranberries (do not thaw)

1⅔ cups granulated white sugar

¾ cup walnut pieces, chopped

½ teaspoon ground cinnamon

½ teaspoon salt

¾ cup plus 2 tablespoons soft white wheat berries

8 tablespoons (1 stick) unsalted butter, melted and cooled to room temperature, plus additional for greasing the pie plate

2 large eggs, at room temperature

½ teaspoon almond extract

1. Position the rack in the center of the oven; heat the oven to 350°F. Generously butter the inside of a 10-inch pie plate, preferably a glass pie plate.

2. Mix the cranberries, ⅔ cup of the sugar, the walnuts, cinnamon, and ¼ teaspoon of the salt in a large bowl. Pour this mixture into the prepared pie plate, getting every last speck out of the bowl.

3. Put the wheat berries in the large canister; cover and blend at the highest speed to a fine flour, about 1 minute. Add the remaining 1 cup sugar and the remaining ¼ teaspoon salt. Cover and pulse a couple of times to combine.

4. Add the melted butter, eggs, and almond extract. Cover and blend at low speed, repeatedly stopping the machine to scrape down the inside of the canister, or using the tamper, if available, until uniform and smooth, about 20 seconds. Pour the batter over the cranberry mixture in the pie plate.

5. Bake until lightly browned and set without a jiggle, until a toothpick inserted into the "cake" portion on top (without touching the cranberries below) comes out clean, about 40 minutes. Cool in the pie plate on a wire rack for at least 30 minutes, or to room temperature, before slicing into wedges to serve.

NOTE: This pie would also be welcome as a weekend breakfast treat.

PEACH SONKER

Here's another old-school treat, this one from North Carolina. There are hundreds of variations: a rich batter baked over fruit that's been doused with melted butter. But even with all those recipes floating around, we'll bet there's not a one that's from a turbo blender—or that's quite so easy. • MAKES ABOUT 8 SERVINGS

6 large, ripe peaches, peeled, pitted, and thinly sliced

1⅔ cups granulated white sugar

1 tablespoon cornstarch

½ teaspoon ground cinnamon

8 tablespoons (1 stick) unsalted butter, melted and cooled to room temperature, plus additional for greasing the pan

1 cup soft white wheat berries

1½ teaspoons baking powder

½ teaspoon baking soda

¼ teaspoon salt

1 cup regular buttermilk

1 large egg

1 teaspoon pure vanilla extract

1. Position the rack in the center of the oven; heat the oven to 350°F. Generously butter the inside of a 9-inch square baking pan.

2. Mix the peaches, ⅔ cup of the sugar, the cornstarch, and cinnamon in a large bowl. Pour into the prepared pan. Pour the melted butter evenly over the peach mixture.

3. Put the wheat berries in the large canister; cover and blend at the highest speed to a fine flour, about 1 minute. Add the remaining 1 cup sugar as well as the baking powder, baking soda, and salt. Cover and pulse a couple of times to combine.

4. Add the buttermilk, egg, and vanilla. Cover and blend at low speed, repeatedly scraping down the inside of the canister, or using the tamper, if available, until uniform and thick, about 15 seconds. Pour and spread the batter evenly over the peach mixture in the pan.

5. Bake the sonker until browned and set, covering the top with aluminum foil if it is browning too deeply before it sets, about 50 minutes. Cool in the pan on a wire rack for 30 minutes or to room temperature before dishing up with a big spoon into bowls.

SWEET CHERRY CLAFOUTI

If you had a French grandmother, you'd know how wonderful this dessert is. If you didn't, you're about to find out (and wish you'd had one). This easy, thickened, sweet custard is poured over the fresh fruit, then baked until lightly browned. Serve it in bowls by dishing it up by the big spoonful. A little whipped cream wouldn't be out of place.

MAKES ABOUT 6 SERVINGS

Unsalted butter, for greasing the pan

1½ pounds pitted sweet cherries (see Note) or one 16-ounce can of pitted sweet cherries, drained

⅔ cup soft white wheat berries

1⅓ cups whole milk

¾ cup granulated white sugar

3 large eggs

1 teaspoon pure vanilla extract

¼ teaspoon salt

⅛ teaspoon almond extract

1. Position the rack in the middle of the oven; heat the oven to 375°F. Generously butter the inside of a 9-inch square baking dish or a shallow, 2-quart, oval baking dish. Pour the cherries in the prepared pan.

2. Put the wheat berries in the large canister; cover and blend at the highest speed to a fine flour, about 1 minute. Add the milk, sugar, eggs, vanilla, salt, and almond extract. Cover and blend at low speed, scraping down the inside of the canister once, until smooth like a pancake batter, about 20 seconds. Pour the batter over the cherries, taking care not to dislodge them too much.

3. Bake the clafouti until set and firm, puffed and lightly browned, about 40 minutes. Cool in the pan on a wire baking rack for at least 30 minutes or to room temperature before serving.

NOTE: Up your game by using 1w¾ pounds sweet cherries with the pits intact. French pastry chefs claim the pits offer a slight bitterness that better balances the sweet custard. But watch out for your teeth— and warn your guests!

MUFFINS, SCONES, & QUICK BREADS

Now that you're making cakes and crisps in the turbo blender, it's a short step to all sorts of baked treats. So here's a set of recipes that'll do you right morning, afternoon, and evening: all sorts of easy muffins and quick breads, a few tender scones, and even a recipe for (whole grain!) popovers.

MUFFINS, SCONES, & QUICK BREADS

ALMOST ALL OF THESE RECIPES ADHERE TO THAT SAME TWO-STEP TECHNIQUE USED IN SOME OF THE CAKES: WHEAT BERRIES AND OTHER DRY INGREDIENTS IN THE CANISTER, FOLLOWED BY LIQUID INGREDIENTS.

Almost all are whirred up separately in two batches and mixed in a bowl on the counter-top. But before we get to the recipes, let's lay out some of the road rules.

A BAKING CHECKLIST

1. When you grind the wheat berries, take care that you don't also steam the resulting flour. Yes, it will be warm by the very nature of the machine. But you don't want it hot. Work at the highest speed. Stop the machine and give it a rest for five minutes or so if you find the flour is steaming a lot.

2. Baking powder and baking soda have a shelf life: about nine months for baking powder, a year for baking soda—*if* you live in a relatively dry climate. Excessive humidity can compromise their effectiveness.

   • To test baking powder, put 1 teaspoon in a small bowl and add ⅓ cup very hot tap water. It should instantly foam.

   • To test baking soda, put ¼ teaspoon in a small bowl and add 2 teaspoons vinegar. It should froth.

   • If either fails the test, throw out the can or box and buy fresh.

3. We don't use paper or foil muffin cups. We attained a better crumb and texture when we greased the muffin indentations to let the fairly sturdy batters come in direct contact

with the increasingly hot metal. Without the insulation of the paper cup, the sides of the muffins set before their centers, allowing the latter to continue to rise. But—and here's the big caveat—you have to grease those indentations well for the muffins to come out. Yes, you can use paper muffin cups, but understand that your results may be, well, flatter, than ours and may take a few extra minutes to bake. And you still need to grease these paper cups to get perfect muffins every time. Do not use foil cups.

4. Fill the indentations in the muffin pan pretty full with batter, at least three-quarters, or maybe almost to the top. Many traditional muffin recipes direct you to fill the inden-tations about two-thirds full. But we're working with whole grain batters that don't have quite the loft of less nourishing fare.

5. Real buttermilk is, by nature, a low-fat product. The fat from the cream went to make butter so buttermilk is the leftover. But modern buttermilk isn't necessarily "real" buttermilk. Modern, North American buttermilk is a cultured dairy product, about like a thinned-out yogurt. It can come in low-fat or even fat-free varieties, based on the milk used to produce the cultured results. That said, if you shop at high-end supermarkets, you might find the original buttermilk in the dairy case, not cultured at all, much thinner than what we've come to expect. We tested these recipes with modern buttermilk, the cultured sort. We suggest you follow suit.

THE STANDARD MUFFIN PAN

Throughout, we call for a "standard" pan, but the mere notion of such a thing is not as simple as you might think. There is no standardization. We mean a pan with indentations that are between 2 ½ and 3 ½ inches in diameter at the top, tapering slightly to the bottom. These indentations hold about 3 ½ ounces of batter (or somewhere between ⅔ cup and 1 cup). We never call for jumbo or mini muffin pans.

Some pans sold fairly regularly in North America are slightly smaller, holding about ½ cup batter in each indentation. If you have such a pan, you can make a few more muffins in a second batch after cooling the pan at room temperature for 15 minutes or so. Reduce the baking time by about 25 percent for these slightly smaller muffins.

STORING THE RESULTS

Most of these baked goods freeze well. Once cooled to room temperature, put the muffins, the whole loaf of quick bread, or the scones in a zip-closed bag, seal well, and store in the freezer for up to 4 months. If desired, you can even slice the quick bread into smaller sections for freezing. Thaw the baked goods out of the bag on the countertop for 15 or 20 minutes—or warm them on a baking sheet in a 200°F oven for 10 minutes or so.

However, if the muffins or quick breads have a crunchy topping, they won't freeze well. These should be stored in a sealed container at room temperature for a couple of days.

Most of the crunchy toppings throughout this chapter are again mix-and-match affairs: feel free to put this oat crunch topping on that muffin—or sometimes even on a quick bread.

SO GET OUT the baking powder and baking soda to get some delicate and delicious baked goods out of your turbo blender. Just don't blame us when your freezer's full.

BUTTERMILK MUFFINS WITH A LEMON GLAZE

These simple muffins are wonderfully tender, sport a delicate crumb, and have just the right sweet/sour contrast. In other words, they're a great example of what the turbo blender can do for baked goods. Of course, you can enjoy the muffins without the glaze. If so, break out the good preserves. • MAKES ABOUT 12 MUFFINS

FOR THE MUFFINS

2¼ cups soft white wheat berries

5 tablespoons granulated white sugar

1 tablespoon baking powder

½ teaspoon salt

1⅔ cups regular buttermilk, at room temperature

3 large eggs, at room temperature

5 tablespoons (½ stick plus 1 tablespoon) unsalted butter, melted and cooled to room temperature, plus additional for greasing the pan

2 teaspoons pure vanilla extract

FOR THE GLAZE

1 cup confectioners' sugar

2 to 3 tablespoons fresh lemon juice

1. To make the muffins, position the rack in the center of the oven; heat the oven to 400°F. Lightly but evenly butter the twelve indentations of a standard muffin pan.

2. Put the wheat berries in the large canister; cover and blend at the highest speed to a fine flour, about 1 minute. Add the granulated white sugar, baking powder, and salt; cover and pulse a few times until uniform. Pour the flour mixture into a large bowl.

3. Put the buttermilk, eggs, melted butter, and vanilla in the large canister. Cover and blend at low speed until smooth. Pour over the flour mixture and stir until smooth. Divide the batter among the prepared muffin pan indentations.

4. Bake until a toothpick inserted into the center of a muffin comes out clean, about 12 minutes. Cool in the pan on a wire rack for 5 minutes, then turn out and continue cooling to room temperature, about 1 hour.

5. To make the glaze, put the confectioners' sugar in a large bowl. Add 2 teaspoons of the lemon juice and stir well. Continue stirring in more lemon juice in ½-teaspoon increments until the glaze can be drizzled but is not runny. Either drizzle over the top of each muffin or dip the muffin tops in the glaze to coat them evenly. Set, glazed side up, on a wire rack for 5 minutes to let the glaze set.

NOTE: Why do we use baking powder when in fact there's acid in the batter and we could simply use baking soda? We want the extra oomph that baking powder provides to get a better rise.

BLUEBERRY MUFFINS

These blueberry muffins include some oats for a little more body, a little more chew—and thus a better contrast to the blueberries. Use only fresh, not frozen. The latter are too wet once thawed to make a successful muffin with this formula. • MAKES ABOUT 12 MUFFINS

1⅓ cups soft white wheat berries

½ cup granulated white sugar

⅓ cup old-fashioned rolled oats (do not use quick-cooking or steel-cut oats)

1 tablespoon baking powder

½ teaspoon salt

¾ cup regular buttermilk, at room temperature

8 tablespoons (1 stick) unsalted butter, melted and cooled to room temperature, plus additional for greasing the pan

1 large egg, at room temperature

1 teaspoon pure vanilla extract

1½ cups fresh blueberries (a little over 5 ounces)

1. Position the rack in the center of the oven; heat the oven to 375°F. Lightly but evenly butter the twelve indentations of a standard muffin pan.

2. Put the wheat berries in the large canister; cover and blend to a fine flour, about 1 minute. Add the sugar, oats, baking powder, and salt; cover and pulse until combined. Pour the flour mixture into a large bowl.

3. Pour the buttermilk, melted butter, egg, and vanilla into the large canister. Cover and blend at low speed until smooth, about 10 seconds. Pour over the flour mixture and stir until smooth. Gently fold in the berries with a rubber spatula until uniform. Divide the batter evenly among the prepared muffin pan indentations.

4. Bake until lightly browned and puffed, until a toothpick or cake tester inserted into the center of a muffin comes out clean, about 15 minutes. Cool in the pan on a wire rack for 5 minutes, then turn out the muffins and continue cooling on the wire rack for at least 15 minutes or until at room temperature.

GLUTEN-FREE BLUEBERRY MUFFINS

Look no farther for the best gluten-free muffins! Because the blender can grind the oats and rice so finely, we can get a great crumb in these moist but light muffins. They won't rise like wheat muffins but they will be tender and satisfying. You'll need plenty of butter!
MAKES ABOUT 12 MUFFINS

3 tablespoons certified gluten-free old-fashioned rolled oats

3 tablespoons sliced almonds

3 tablespoons yellow cornmeal

2½ tablespoons raw long-grain brown rice

6 tablespoons packed dark brown sugar

6 tablespoons cornstarch

2 teaspoons baking powder

½ teaspoon baking soda

½ teaspoon salt

⅔ cup regular buttermilk

¼ cup vegetable or canola oil (see Note), plus additional for greasing the pan

1 large egg

1 cup fresh blueberries (about 4½ ounces)

1. Position the rack in the center of the oven; heat the oven to 400°F. Generously oil the twelve indentations of a standard muffin pan.

2. Put the oats, almonds, cornmeal, and rice in the large canister; cover and blend at the highest speed to a powdery flour, about 1 minute. Add the sugar, cornstarch, baking powder, baking soda, and salt; cover and blend at the highest speed until well combined, about 10 seconds.

3. Add the buttermilk, oil, and egg. Cover and blend at low speed until thick and smooth. Remove the canister from the motor housing, add the blueberries and gently fold them into the batter with a rubber spatula. Set aside, covered, at room temperature for 10 minutes so the batter can begin to thicken.

4. Divide the batter evenly among the prepared indentations in the muffin pan. Bake until well browned and a toothpick or cake tester inserted into one of the muffins without touching a blueberry comes out with a few moist crumbs attached, about 15 minutes. Cool in the pan on a wire rack for 5 minutes, then turn the muffins out onto the rack and continue cooling for at least 5 minutes or to room temperature.

NOTE: Take these to the next level by substituting a toasted nut oil like walnut oil or pecan oil for the vegetable oil.

LEMONADE MUFFINS

Lemonade concentrate gives the batter a decided spark of flavor, far better than mere lemon juice. Yogurt will give the muffins a more delicate flavor; sour cream, a slightly more powerful pop. • MAKES 12 MUFFINS

1⅓ cups soft white wheat berries

2 tablespoons granulated white sugar

1½ teaspoons baking soda

½ teaspoon baking powder

¼ teaspoon salt

½ cup thawed, frozen lemonade concentrate (see Note)

4 tablespoons (½ stick) unsalted butter, melted and cooled to room temperature, plus additional for greasing the pan

2 tablespoons plain, regular yogurt or regular sour cream

1 large egg, at room temperature

1. Position the rack in the center of the oven; heat the oven to 375°F. Lightly butter the twelve indentations of a standard muffin pan.

2. Put the wheat berries in the large canister; cover and blend at the highest speed to a fine flour, about 1 minute. Add the sugar, baking soda, baking powder, and salt; cover and pulse until well combined. Pour the flour mixture into a large bowl.

3. Put the lemonade concentrate, melted butter, yogurt or sour cream, and vanilla in the large canister. Cover and blend at low speed until smooth, about 10 seconds. Pour over the flour mixture and stir to form a thick, evenly moistened batter. Divide the batter among the prepared muffin pan indentations.

4. Bake until puffed and set, until a toothpick or cake tester inserted into the center of one muffin comes out clean, 15 to 18 minutes. Cool in the pan on a wire rack for 10 minutes, then turn the muffins out onto the rack and continue cooling for 15 minutes or to room temperature.

NOTE: Do not use low-sugar or sugar-free lemonade concentrates.

JAM MUFFINS WITH A STREUSEL TOPPING

By mixing jam into the muffin batter, we can get a more decided chew in the texture—and lots of flavor! Choose any jam you like, even orange marmalade. But avoid preserves (too many chunks of fruit) or jelly (not enough flavor for these muffins). If you omit the crunchy topping, serve the muffins with the same kind of jam you used to make them.

MAKES 12 MUFFINS

FOR THE MUFFINS

2 cups soft white wheat berries

¾ cup granulated white sugar

2 teaspoons baking soda

1 teaspoon baking powder

½ teaspoon salt

1 cup regular buttermilk, at room temperature

½ cup jam or marmalade of your choice

6 tablespoons (¾ stick) unsalted butter, melted and cooled to room temperature, plus additional for greasing the pan

2 large eggs, at room temperature

½ teaspoon pure vanilla extract

FOR THE TOPPING

¼ cup all-purpose flour

¼ cup granulated white sugar

1 teaspoon ground cinnamon

4 tablespoons (½ stick) cold unsalted butter, cut into small bits

1. To start the muffins, position the rack in the center of the oven; heat the oven to 400°F. Lightly but evenly butter the twelve indentations of a standard muffin pan.

2. Put the wheat berries in the large canister; cover and blend at the highest speed to a fine flour, about 1 minute. Add the sugar, baking soda, baking powder, and salt; cover and pulse until uniform. Pour the flour mixture into a large bowl.

3. Pour the buttermilk, jam or marmalade, melted butter, eggs, and vanilla into the large canister. Cover and blend at low speed until smooth, about 10 seconds. Pour into the flour mixture and stir until smooth. Divide the batter evenly among the prepared muffin pan indentations.

4. To make the topping, mix the flour, sugar, and cinnamon in a large bowl until uniform. Cut in the butter with a pastry cutter or a fork until the mixture resembles coarse meal. Sprinkle this topping over each muffin, dividing it equally.

5. Bake until puffed and set, until a toothpick or cake tester inserted into one muffin comes out with a few moist crumbs attached, about 15 minutes. Cool in the pan on a wire rack for 5 minutes, then turn the muffins out onto the rack and continue cooling for at least 15 minutes or to room temperature.

CHOCOLATE CAKE MUFFINS WITH A VANILLA GLAZE

These muffins are pretty dense, more cakey than many standard muffins. For a dessert treat, consider skipping the vanilla glaze and serving them with Turbo Blender Whipped Cream (page 52).

MAKES 12 MUFFINS

FOR THE MUFFINS

1⅔ cup soft white wheat berries

½ cup granulated white sugar

½ cup packed dark brown sugar

⅓ cup unsweetened cocoa powder

1 tablespoon baking powder

½ teaspoon salt

1½ cups whole or 2 percent milk, at room temperature

8 tablespoons (1 stick) unsalted butter, melted and cooled to room temperature, plus additional for greasing the pan

2 large eggs, at room temperature

2 teaspoons pure vanilla extract

FOR THE GLAZE

2 tablespoons very hot water

2 teaspoons light corn syrup

2 teaspoons pure vanilla extract

⅛ teaspoon salt

At least 1¼ cups confectioners' sugar

1. Position the rack in the center of the oven; heat the oven to 400°F. Lightly but evenly butter the twelve indentations of a standard muffin pan.

2. Put the wheat berries in the large canister; cover and blend at the highest speed to a fine flour, about 1 minute. Add the granulated white sugar, brown sugar, cocoa powder, baking powder, and salt. Cover and pulse until uniform; pour into a large bowl.

3. Pour the milk, melted butter, eggs, and vanilla in the large canister. Cover and blend at low speed until smooth, about 10 seconds. Pour into the flour mixture and stir until smooth. Divide the batter evenly among the prepared muffin pan indentations.

4. Bake until puffed and set, until a toothpick or cake tester inserted into the center of one muffin comes out clean, about 12 minutes. Cool in the pan on a wire rack for 5 minutes, then turn the muffins out onto the rack and continue cooling to room temperature, about 1 hour.

5. To glaze the muffins, whisk the hot water, corn syrup, vanilla, and salt in a medium bowl until uniform. Add 1¼ cups of the confectioners' sugar and stir with a wooden spoon to form a glaze that can be drizzled without running, adding more confectioners' sugar in 1-tablespoon increments to achieve the right consistency. Drizzle this glaze generously over the tops of the cooled muffins.

NOTE: To turn these into Mexican chocolate muffins, add 1½ teaspoons ground cinnamon, ¼ teaspoon freshly grated nutmeg (or ⅛ teaspoon ground nutmeg), and ¼ teaspoon almond extract with the milk.

PEANUT BUTTER MUFFINS

These muffins are sturdy enough to pack into school lunches or even a briefcase. (Everybody needs a treat during the day!) They're best with Concord grape jelly—just as a peanut butter sandwich is! • MAKES 12 MUFFINS

1½ cups soft white wheat berries

½ cup packed light brown sugar

1 tablespoon baking powder

½ teaspoon salt

1¼ cups whole or 2 percent milk, at room temperature

⅔ cup peanut butter (any sort)

6 tablespoons (¾ stick) unsalted butter, melted and cooled to room temperature, plus additional for greasing the pan

1 large egg, at room temperature

2 teaspoons pure vanilla extract

1. Position the rack in the center of the oven; heat the oven to 375°F. Lightly but evenly butter the twelve indentations of a standard muffin pan.

2. Put the wheat berries in the large canister; cover and blend at the highest speed to a fine flour, about 1 minute. Add the sugar, baking powder, and salt; cover and pulse until well combined. Pour the flour mixture into a large bowl.

3. Put the milk, peanut butter, melted butter, egg, and vanilla in the large canister. Cover and blend at low speed until smooth, about 15 seconds. Pour into the flour mixture and stir until an evenly moistened batter forms. Divide the batter among the prepared muffin pan indentations.

4. Bake until puffed and set, until a toothpick or cake tester inserted into one muffin comes out clean, 12 to 15 minutes. Cool in the pan on a wire rack for 5 minutes, then turn the muffins out onto the rack and continue cooling for 15 minutes or to room temperature.

BANANA-ALMOND MUFFINS

This is the muffin equivalent of banana bread, fairly light but with distinct body. They don't keep well on the counter because the oats and bananas compromise the texture quickly. However, they do freeze well. Once cooled, store them in a zip-closed plastic bag in the freezer for up to 4 months. The topping offers a delicate, crunchy contrast.
MAKES 12 MUFFINS

⅓ cup soft white wheat berries

⅓ cup sliced almonds

¾ cup old-fashioned rolled oats (do not use quick-cooking or steel-cut)

3 tablespoons packed light brown sugar

1½ teaspoons baking powder

½ teaspoon baking soda

½ teaspoon ground cinnamon

¼ teaspoon salt

2 medium, ripe bananas, peeled and broken into pieces

2 large eggs

¼ cup vegetable or canola oil, plus additional for greasing the pan

¼ cup whole milk

1. Position the rack in the center of the oven; heat the oven to 400°F. Use an oiled paper

towel to grease the twelve indentations of a standard muffin pan.

2. Put the wheat berries in the large canister; cover and blend at the highest speed to a fine flour, about 30 seconds. Add the almonds; cover and grind at the highest speed until powdery, about 20 seconds. Add the oats, sugar, baking powder, baking soda, cinnamon, and salt; cover and pulse a few times until well combined.

3. Add the bananas, eggs, oil, and milk. Cover and blend at low speed until thick but smooth, almost like thick waffle batter. Remove the canister from the motor housing and set aside, covered, on the counter for 10 minutes to thicken the batter somewhat. Divide the batter evenly among the prepared muffin pan indentations.

4. Bake until puffed and set and a toothpick or cake tester inserted into the center of one muffin comes out clean, about 18 minutes. Cool in the pan on a wire rack for 10 minutes, then turn the muffins out onto the rack and continue cooling for 15 minutes or to room temperature.

DATE-NUT MUFFINS

Forget the date nut bread popular in the '70s. These muffins are lighter and more tender, still packed with lots of date flavor. (They're also whole wheat muffins!) Make sure those dates are soft and moist, rather than dry and fibrous. There's no need for the milk or egg to be at room temperature because the recipe uses oil, not melted butter. • MAKES 12 MUFFINS

1¾ cups soft white wheat berries

½ cup granulated white sugar

1 tablespoon baking powder

½ teaspoon ground cinnamon

½ teaspoon salt

1 cup whole or 2 percent milk

¼ cup canola or vegetable oil, plus additional for greasing the pan

3 tablespoons molasses

1 large egg

2 teaspoons pure vanilla extract

1 cup chopped pitted dates

¾ cup chopped pecans or walnuts

1. Position the rack in the center of the oven; heat the oven to 400°F. Lightly grease twelve indentations of a standard muffin pan.

2. Put the wheat berries in the large canister; cover and blend at the highest speed to a fine flour, about 1 minute. Add the sugar, baking powder, cinnamon, and salt; cover and pulse until combined. Pour into a large bowl.

3. Pour the milk, oil, molasses, egg, and vanilla into the large canister. Cover and blend at low speed until smooth, about 10 seconds. Add the dates and nuts; pulse a couple of times to chop. Pour over the flour mixture and stir to form a thick, evenly moistened batter. Divide the batter among the prepared muffin pan indentations.

4. Bake until puffed and set, until a toothpick or cake tester inserted into one muffin comes out with a few moist crumbs attached, 18 to 20 minutes. Cool in the pan on a wire rack for 10 minutes, then turn the muffins out onto the rack and continue cooling for 10 minutes or to room temperature.

GRAHAM CRACKER MUFFINS

By grinding the graham crackers into the flour we've made in the canister, we can create a muffin equivalent of one of our favorite cookie snacks. But we also add a little jam into the batter—because it's all that classic combo with graham crackers, after all.
MAKES 12 MUFFINS

FOR THE MUFFINS

¾ cup soft white wheat berries

9 large graham crackers (1 sleeve, 4.8 ounces), broken into pieces

1 tablespoon baking powder

½ teaspoon salt

6 tablespoons (¾ stick) unsalted butter, melted and cooled to room temperature, plus additional for greasing the pan

⅓ cup strawberry or Concord grape jam

¼ cup honey

1 large egg, at room temperature

1 teaspoon pure vanilla extract

2 tablespoons old-fashioned rolled oats (do not use instant or steel-cut)

1 tablespoon granulated white sugar

1. Position the rack in the center of the oven; heat the oven to 375°F. Lightly but evenly butter the twelve indentations of a standard muffin pan.

2. Put the wheat berries in the large canister; cover and blend at the highest speed to a fine flour, about 1 minute. Add the graham crackers, baking powder, and salt; cover and pulse several times until the graham crackers are finely ground. Pour the flour mixture into a large bowl.

3. Put the melted butter, jam, honey, egg, and vanilla in the large canister. Cover and blend at low speed until smooth, about 10 seconds. Pour over the flour mixture and stir to form a thick batter. Divide the batter evenly among the prepared muffin pan indentations. Mix the sugar and oats in a small bowl; sprinkle this mixture over each unbaked muffin, dividing it equally.

4. Bake until puffed and set, until a toothpick or cake tester inserted into the center of a muffin comes out clean, 15 to 18 minutes. Cool in the pan on a wire rack for 10 minutes, then turn the muffins out onto the rack and continue cooling for 15 minutes or to room temperature.

CORN MUFFINS

Although these are sweet muffins, not savory, they still might be welcome at a holiday table, particularly alongside a roast turkey or chicken. They also won't rise up as high as traditional muffins. We wanted them a bit denser to give them a "cornier" texture. We wouldn't recommend a topping on them. They just need butter! • MAKES 12 MUFFINS

¾ cup plus 2 tablespoons soft white wheat berries

1⅓ cups yellow cornmeal

¼ cup granulated white sugar

2 teaspoons baking soda

½ teaspoon baking powder

¼ teaspoon salt

1 cup regular buttermilk, at room temperature

⅔ cup regular or low-fat sour cream, at room temperature

5 tablespoons (½ stick plus 1 tablespoon) unsalted butter, melted and cooled to room temperature, plus additional for greasing the pan

2 large eggs, at room temperature

1. Position the rack in the center of the oven; heat the oven to 375°F. Lightly but evenly butter the twelve indentations of a standard muffin pan.

2. Put the wheat berries in the large canister; cover and blend at the highest speed to a fine flour, about 1 minute. Add the cornmeal, sugar, baking soda, baking powder, and salt; cover and pulse until uniform. Pour the flour mixture into a large bowl.

3. Put the buttermilk, sour cream, melted butter, and eggs in the large canister. Cover and blend at low speed until smooth, about 10 seconds. Pour over the flour mixture and stir to form a uniformly moistened batter. Divide the batter evenly among the prepared muffin pan indentations.

4. Bake until puffed and lightly browned, until a toothpick or cake tester inserted into a muffin comes out clean, 15 to 16 minutes. Cool in the pan on a wire rack for 5 minutes, then turn the muffins out onto the rack and continue cooling for at least 15 minutes or to room temperature.

PECAN MUFFINS WITH A CHOCOLATE GLAZE

To make these muffins, you'll need to pulse the pecans in the blender to grind them a little finer than a mere chopping on a cutting board would do. Their characteristic flavor can then permeate the batter. • MAKES 12 MUFFINS

FOR THE MUFFINS

1¼ cups plus 2 tablespoons soft white wheat berries

⅓ cup packed dark brown sugar

2 teaspoons baking soda

½ teaspoon baking powder

½ teaspoon salt

½ cup regular buttermilk, at room temperature

2 large eggs, at room temperature

¼ cup maple syrup, preferably Grade B or 2

4 tablespoons (½ stick) unsalted butter, melted and cooled to room temperature, plus additional for greasing the pan

1 teaspoon pure vanilla extract

1½ cups pecan pieces

FOR THE GLAZE

2 ounces unsweetened chocolate, chopped

¼ cup water

2 tablespoons light corn syrup

¼ teaspoon salt

2½ cups confectioners' sugar

1 teaspoon pure vanilla extract

1. To make the muffins, position the rack in the center of the oven; heat the oven to 400°F. Lightly but evenly butter the twelve indentations of a standard muffin pan.

2. Put the wheat berries in the large canister; cover and blend at the highest speed to a fine flour, about 1 minute. Add the brown sugar, baking soda, baking powder, and salt; cover and pulse until uniform. Pour the flour mixture into a large bowl.

3. Pour the buttermilk, eggs, maple syrup, melted butter, and vanilla into the large canister. Cover and blend at low speed until smooth, about 10 seconds. Add the pecans and pulse once or twice until uniformly distributed. Pour over the flour mixture and stir to form a thick batter. Divide the batter evenly among the prepared muffin pan indentations.

4. Bake until a toothpick or cake tester inserted into the center of a muffin comes out clean, about 15 minutes. Cool in the pan on a wire rack for 10 minutes, then turn the muffins out onto the rack and continue cooling to room temperature, about 1 hour.

5. To make the glaze, put the chopped chocolate in a large bowl. Combine the water, corn syrup, and salt in a small saucepan. Set over medium-high heat and bring just to a simmer, stirring often. Pour over the chocolate in the bowl and stir until melted and uniform. Set aside to cool for 5 minutes.

6. Stir in the confectioners' sugar and vanilla to make slightly thick glaze. Dip a muffin upside down in this glaze, coating the top thoroughly and evenly. Set on a wire rack and dip the remainder of the muffins. If desired, let the glaze harden a bit on the tops for 5 minutes, then dip them all again for a thicker coating.

CHOCOLATE CHIP SCONES

Here are classic scones, ready for an afternoon snack or a weekend breakfast. Note that the milk and egg in this recipe are *not* at room temperature, despite the presence of butter. If some of that butter clumps, the scones will have more of the classic texture, little bits of butter melted throughout the crumb. Also note that the all-purpose flour is given as a range here. You want to stir in just enough to reach the desired consistency—and the amount will be affected by the day's humidity as well as the residual moisture content of the other ingredients. • MAKES 8 SCONES

1¼ cups soft white wheat berries

½ cup packed light brown sugar

2½ teaspoons baking powder

½ teaspoon ground cinnamon

½ teaspoon salt

8 tablespoons (1 stick) unsalted butter, melted and cooled to room temperature

½ cup whole milk

1 large egg

2 teaspoons pure vanilla extract

1 cup semisweet or bittersweet chocolate chips (see Note)

Up to ¾ cup all-purpose flour

Granulated white sugar for garnishing, if desired

1. Position the rack in the center of the oven; heat the oven to 375°F. Line a large, rimmed baking sheet with parchment paper or a silicone baking mat.

2. Put the wheat berries in the large canister; cover and blend at the highest speed to a fine flour, about 1 minute. Add the brown sugar, baking powder, cinnamon, and salt; cover and pulse until uniform. Pour the flour mixture into a large bowl.

3. Put the melted butter, milk, egg, and vanilla in the large canister. Cover and blend at low speed until smooth, about 20 seconds. Pour into the flour mixture, add the chocolate chips, and stir to form a wet, sticky dough. Stir in the additional all-purpose flour in ¼-cup increments, adding less and less with each addition, just until a slightly sticky but still smooth dough forms.

4. Turn the dough out onto the prepared baking sheet and form into a 10-inch circle. Cut the circle into 8 wedges, then pull these apart to separate them by an inch or two. Sprinkle each with granulated white sugar, if desired.

5. Bake the scones until puffed and light brown, 18 to 20 minutes. Cool on the baking sheet on a wire rack for 5 minutes. Using a large metal spatula, transfer the scones directly to the wire rack and cool for at least 15 minutes more or to room temperature.

NOTE: You can omit the chocolate chips, but they do leach a little necessary fat into the scones. Substitute ½ cup finely chopped nuts.

DATE-WALNUT SCONES

These scones are denser than those in the previous recipe, so these are a better vehicle for well-stocked berry or fruit preserves.

MAKES 8 SCONES

1¼ cups soft white wheat berries

¼ cup plus 1 tablespoon granulated white sugar

1½ teaspoons baking powder

½ teaspoon baking soda

½ teaspoon salt

8 tablespoons (1 stick) unsalted butter, melted and cooled to room temperature

½ cup regular buttermilk

2 large eggs

½ cup walnut pieces

7 large dates, preferably Medjool dates, pitted

Up to ¾ cup all-purpose flour

1 teaspoon ground cinnamon

1. Position the rack in the center of the oven; heat the oven to 375°F. Line a large, rimmed baking sheet with parchment paper or a silicone baking mat.

2. Put the wheat berries in the large canister; cover and blend at the highest speed to a fine flour, about 1 minute. Add ¼ cup sugar, the baking powder, baking soda, and salt; cover and pulse to blend. Pour the flour mixture into a large bowl.

3. Put the melted butter, buttermilk, eggs, walnuts, and dates in the large canister. Cover and pulse until the nuts and dates are roughly chopped but not pureed.

4. Pour into the flour mixture and stir to form a sticky dough. Stir in ¼ cup all-purpose flour and then less and less flour with each addition until the dough is only slightly sticky, pliable, and smooth.

5. Turn the dough out onto the prepared baking sheet and form into a 10-inch circle. Cut the circle into 8 wedges and separate these from each other by an inch or two. Mix the remaining 1 tablespoon sugar and the cinnamon in a small bowl; sprinkle over each wedge, dividing it equally.

6. Bake the scones until brown, puffed, and set, about 18 minutes. Cool on the baking sheet on a wire rack for 10 minutes. Using a large metal spatula, transfer the scones directly to the wire rack. Cool for 15 minutes more or to room temperature.

CARROT-RAISIN SCONES

Think of these as a cross between carrot cake and scones. (Our recipes get to be a little whimsical sometimes!) These muffins are denser than carrot cake, of course, more like traditional scones, if with a cakey crumb. Look for shredded carrots at the salad bar of your supermarket. Serve these scones with cream cheese for the full experience.

MAKES 8 SCONES

1¼ cups soft white wheat berries

¼ cup granulated white sugar

1 tablespoon baking powder

½ teaspoon ground cinnamon

½ teaspoon salt

½ cup regular buttermilk

½ cup shredded carrot

6 tablespoons (¾ stick) unsalted butter, melted and cooled to room temperature

¼ cup raisins

¼ cup pecan pieces

1 large egg, at room temperature

Up to ¾ cup all-purpose flour

1. Position the rack in the center of the oven; heat the oven to 375°F. Line a large rimmed baking sheet with parchment paper or a silicone baking mat.

2. Put the wheat berries in the large canister; cover and blend at the highest speed to a fine flour, about 1 minute. Add the sugar, baking powder, cinnamon, and salt; cover and pulse until uniform. Pour into a large bowl.

3. Put the buttermilk, carrot, melted butter, raisins, pecans, and egg in the large canister. Cover and pulse 2 to 3 times until the carrots and nuts are roughly chopped but not pureed.

4. Pour into the bowl with the flour mixture and stir to form a sticky dough. Stir in ¼ cup all-purpose flour, then less and less with each further addition, until a slightly sticky, pliable, and smooth dough forms.

5. Turn the dough out onto the prepared baking sheet and form into a 10-inch circle. Cut the circle into 8 wedges; separate each wedge by an inch or two.

6. Bake the scones until lightly browned and set, 18 to 20 minutes. Cool on the baking sheet on a wire rack for 5 minutes. Using a large metal spatula, transfer the scones directly onto the wire rack. Cool for at least another 15 minutes or to room temperature.

NOTE: Don't grind the nuts—simply chop them until they're evenly distributed.

BANANA BREAD

What's with all the banana bread haters? Maybe they've had cold, stale banana bread. As you probably know, it's never better than during the first hour or so after it comes out of the oven. Warm, it cries out for butter! However, if you've still got half a loaf the next morning, it toasts beautifully, either in a toaster oven or on a baking sheet under the broiler. • MAKES ONE 9-INCH LOAF

1½ cups soft white wheat berries

½ cup granulated white sugar

½ cup packed light brown sugar

1 teaspoon baking soda

½ teaspoon ground cinnamon

¼ teaspoon baking powder

¼ teaspoon salt

3 medium, very ripe bananas, peeled and cut into chunks

⅓ cup canola or vegetable oil, plus additional for greasing the pan

2 large eggs

1 teaspoon pure vanilla extract

½ cup walnut pieces or sliced almonds

2 tablespoons all-purpose flour

1. Position the rack in the center of the oven; heat the oven to 375°F. Generously oil the inside of a 9 x 5-inch loaf pan.

2. Put the wheat berries in the large canister; cover and blend at the highest speed to a fine flour, about 1 minute. Add the white sugar, brown sugar, baking soda, cinnamon, baking powder, and salt; cover and pulse until uniform. Pour the flour mixture into a large bowl.

(continued)

QUICK GINGERBREAD

No, it's not traditional gingerbread. But boy, is it fast and delicious! It's perfect when guests drop in. But one caution: the batter is fairly thick. Make sure you spread it evenly in the pan. • MAKES ONE 9-INCH LOAF

2 cups soft white wheat berries

¾ cup packed dark brown sugar

1 tablespoon ground dried ginger

2 teaspoons baking soda

1½ teaspoons ground cinnamon

½ teaspoon ground cloves

¼ teaspoon ground allspice, optional

1 cup regular buttermilk, at room temperature

8 tablespoons (1 stick) unsalted butter, melted and cooled to room temperature, plus additional for greasing the pan

⅓ cup molasses

2 large eggs, at room temperature

2 teaspoons pure vanilla extract

2 tablespoons all-purpose flour

1. Position the rack in the center of the oven; heat the oven to 375°F. Generously butter the inside of a 9 x 5-inch loaf pan.

2. Put the wheat berries in the large canister; cover and blend at the highest speed to a fine flour, about 1 minute. Add the sugar, ginger, baking soda, cinnamon, cloves, and allspice, if using. Cover and pulse until uniform; pour the flour mixture into a large bowl.

3. Pour the buttermilk, melted butter, molasses, eggs, and vanilla into the large canister. Cover and blend until smooth. Pour over the flour mixture and whisk to form a batter. Whisk in the flour until dissolved. Pour and

3. Put the bananas, oil, eggs, and vanilla in the large canister. Cover and blend at low speed until smooth, about 10 seconds. Add the nuts and pulse once or twice to lightly chop. Pour over the flour mixture; stir to create a thick batter. Add the flour and stir until dissolved. Pour and scrape the batter into the prepared pan, gently smoothing it out to an even depth.

4. Bake the banana bread until lightly browned and set, until a toothpick or cake tester inserted into the center of the loaf come out clean, 40 to 45 minutes. Cool in the pan on a wire rack for 5 minutes, then turn the loaf out onto the rack and continue cooling for at least 10 minutes or to room temperature.

scrape the batter into the prepared loaf pan, gently smoothing to an even depth.

4. Bake the gingerbread until browned and set, until a toothpick or cake tester inserted into the center of the loaf comes out with a few moist crumbs attached, 40 to 45 minutes. Cool in the pan on a wire rack for 5 minutes, then turn the loaf out onto the rack and continue cooling for at least 10 minutes or to room temperature.

CHOCOLATE BUTTERMILK QUICK BREAD

There are no eggs in this quick bread, so it has a denser, chewier texture, more like a quick bread version of a brownie. Do not overbake the loaf. The chocolate can singe and turn bitter; the texture can dry out too much and become sandy. It will continue to "bake" a bit as it cools on the rack.

MAKES ONE 9-INCH LOAF

1¼ cups soft white wheat berries

½ cup unsweetened cocoa powder

1 teaspoon baking soda

½ teaspoon salt

1 cup granulated white sugar

1 cup regular buttermilk

⅓ cup canola or vegetable oil, plus additional for oiling the pan

1 teaspoon pure vanilla extract

1. Position the rack in the center of the oven; heat the oven to 350°F. Generously grease the inside of a 9 x 5-inch loaf pan with a paper towel dabbed with some oil.

2. Put the wheat berries in the large canister; cover and blend at the highest speed to a fine flour, about 1 minute. Add the cocoa powder, baking soda, and salt; cover and pulse until uniform. Add the sugar, buttermilk, oil, and vanilla; cover and pulse repeatedly, scraping down the inside of the canister several times, or using the tamper, if available, to create a thick, smooth batter. Pour and scrape the batter into the prepared loaf pan, smoothing it to an even depth.

3. Bake the bread until set and a toothpick or cake tester inserted into the center of the cake comes out with a few moist crumbs attached, about 40 minutes. Cool in the pan on a wire rack for no more than 5 minutes, then turn the loaf out onto the rack and continue cooling for at least 10 minutes, or to room temperature.

SOUR CREAM CHOCOLATE CHIP QUICK BREAD

This is the most sturdy loaf among our quick breads: a little sour, still fairly sweet, with lots of chocolate chips, about as many as it can handle. • MAKES ONE 9-INCH LOAF

1¾ cups soft white wheat berries

⅔ cup granulated white sugar

2 teaspoons baking soda

½ teaspoon baking powder

½ teaspoon salt

1 cup regular sour cream, at room temperature

⅔ cup whole or 2 percent milk, at room temperature

(continued)

6 tablespoons (¾ stick) unsalted butter, melted and cooled to room temperature, plus additional for greasing the pan

2 large eggs, at room temperature

1 teaspoon pure vanilla extract

1¼ cups semisweet or bittersweet chocolate chips

6 tablespoons all-purpose flour

1. Position the rack in the center of the oven; heat the oven to 375°F. Generously butter the inside of a 9 x 5-inch loaf pan.

2. Put the wheat berries in the large canister; cover and blend at the highest speed to a fine flour, about 1 minute 15 seconds. Add the sugar, baking soda, baking powder, and salt; cover and pulse to combine. Pour the flour mixture into a large bowl.

3. Put the sour cream, milk, melted butter, eggs, and vanilla in the large canister. Cover and blend at low speed until smooth, about 10 seconds. Pour over the flour mixture and stir to combine until there are no dry pockets. Add the chocolate chips and all-purpose flour. Stir until there is no dry flour remaining in the bowl and the batter is fairly thick, with the chips evenly distributed throughout. Pour and scrape the batter into the prepared pan, smoothing it to an even depth.

4. Bake the bread until lightly browned and set, until a toothpick or cake tester inserted into the center of the loaf comes out clean, 40 to 45 minutes. Cool in the pan on a wire rack for 10 minutes, then turn the loaf out onto the rack and continue cooling for at least 15 minutes or to room temperature.

POPOVERS

Can you believe it? From a turbo blender? And whole grain popovers at that? What a treat! You'll need a popover pan for this recipe, not a standard muffin pan. The pan has fairly deep cups, each between 2½ and 3 inches in diameter with a similar depth and sometimes a slight taper. Look for it at specialty cookware stores and their online outlets.

MAKES 6 POPOVERS

1 cup soft white wheat berries

½ teaspoon salt

1 cup whole milk, at room temperature

2 large eggs, at room temperature

2 tablespoons unsalted butter, melted and cooled to room temperature, plus additional for greasing the pan

1. Position the rack in the center of the oven; heat the oven to 400°F.

2. Very generously butter the six indentations in a standard popover pan. Set the pan in the heated oven for 10 minutes.

3. Meanwhile, put the wheat berries and salt in the large canister; cover and blend to a fine flour, about 1 minute. Add the milk, eggs, and melted butter; cover and blend at low speed until very smooth, about 20 seconds.

4. Divide the batter evenly among the prepared, hot indentations. Bake the popovers until puffed and golden, about 30 minutes. Cool in the pan on a wire rack for 5 minutes before turning the popovers out onto the rack and continuing to cool for 5 to 15 minutes. Serve warm.

PANCAKES & WAFFLES

THIS ONE IS CERTAINLY NOT A CHAPTER OF DESSERTS, BUT WE COULDN'T RESIST. AFTER ALL, WE CAN APPLY THAT SAME TWO-STEP TECHNIQUE—GRINDING THE FLOUR TO MIX WITH OTHER DRY INGREDIENTS, THEN BLENDING IN THE WET STUFF UNTIL SMOOTH—TO ALMOST ALL OF THESE SIMPLE BATTERS.

AND THEN WE MAKE THEM BETTER! WE'RE MAKING WHOLE GRAIN PANCAKES AND WAFFLES, THE BEST WE CAN GIVE OUR FAMILY AND FRIENDS. THE TEXTURE WILL BE MORE SUBSTANTIAL, A BETTER VEHICLE TO BIG FLAVORS (AS WELL AS BUTTER AND SYRUP).

We can make these batters easier, too! We're not dirtying bowls or mixers. Instead, we're creating almost all of these batters right in the blender canister. Yes, they'll get thick. You'll need to either use the tamper or stop the machine repeatedly to scrape down and reposition the mixture inside, but you'll end up with delicate, light breakfast fare. (Or some pretty good dinners, too!)

THREE TIPS

1. If you've got company around and want to make your morning even easier, drag out the dry ingredients the night before. Don't grind the wheat berries. The resulting flour can either get soggy with humidity or dry out overnight. But with things ready to go, you'll have a faster breakfast the next morning.

2. We usually pour the batter straight from the canister onto the griddle (for pancakes) or into the waffle iron. That said, this is a whole grain batter, so it can tighten up a bit as it sits on the countertop. If you find it's getting stiff, add 1 tablespoon milk or buttermilk (whichever the recipe requires), cover, and blend again at low speed until smooth. You want a pourable but still not soupy texture.

3. Some of these batters also call for a little additional all-purpose flour. We found that they got too dense with only whole wheat flour. So we added a touch of the more standard stuff to give them a lighter, less chewy texture.

TOPPINGS

Yes, maple syrup—of course. We tend to go for Grade A (or 1) *dark amber* for our breakfasts because we like more flavor than the light or medium amber affords. But why stop at maple syrup? Ever tried sorghum syrup? It's rich and malty, not quite as sweet, with a slightly herbal finish. Or go all out and search online for suppliers of birch syrup from Alaska. It has a distinctly mineral flavor with grassy and pronounced herbal notes. Or steer clear of syrups entirely and enjoy these pancakes and waffles with your favorite jam or preserves. Butter's an essential, if you do. And while we're not fans of whipped cream on pancakes or waffles, you might be—and you know where to find the easiest recipe around (see page 52).

PANCAKES

HERE'S A COLLECTION OF PANCAKE RECIPES, EVERYTHING FROM BUTTERMILK TO LEMON POPPY SEED, FROM GLUTEN-FREE TO OAT AND HONEY, FROM RICOTTA TO CHOCOLATE.

And there are three specialty "Pancakes" at the end: Dutch babies and one pancake coffee cake (we'll explain that later).

There's a lot of repetition in these recipes. Sorry about that. Frankly, this whole section is really about the ratios. The technique is the same over and over.

As we've stated in other places, cold milk and eggs can shock the butter and turn it into firm, little specks. To avoid this problem, most ingredients must be at room temperature. Our advice is to stumble to the kitchen, measure them out, and go take your shower or get ready for breakfast. They'll be perfect when you're ready.

THE RIGHT COOKWARE

In general, pancakes should be made on a griddle or in a large, flat-bottomed skillet, preferably either a giant, arm-breaking, well-seasoned, cast-iron skillet or an equally large nonstick one. If you use nonstick cookware, you must also use nonstick-safe spatulas to keep from nicking the special surface.

In either case (and even if you're using a nonstick pan), you'll want to grease the griddle or skillet before you heat it and then again between batches. We find the easiest way to get the job done once the surface is hot is to wad up a paper towel, pick it up with (nonstick-safe) kitchen tongs, spray the paper with nonstick cooking spray, and then rub it quickly across the hot surface. (Don't use a baking spray with flour in the mix.) Of course, you can also melt butter on the griddle or in the skillet, but make sure you smear it around to get an even coating, probably employing that same paper-towel-kitchen-tong fandango.

THE RIGHT SET

Plan on 4-inch pancakes. The recipe will tell you how much batter to use. Pour the pools of batter into the pan, then watch them carefully. They should spread without running. And they should begin to form a bubble or two fairly quickly, certainly within the first minute. You're looking for bubbles that rise and pop open but do not close up, leaving a little hole behind. When the surface is dotted with a few (not a lot), check under one pancake to see if it's done, lifting an edge off the hot surface with a spatula (nonstick-safe if needed). If it's browned, flip it over and continue cooking for about 1 minute, until browned on the opposite side.

Remember that pancakes are thin and can sometimes cook too quickly, burning on the outside before setting in the middle. Keep the heat under the griddle or skillet at a moderate level, dropping it down to medium-low once you're rolling into the second batch. However, if the heat gets too low, the pancakes will not cook in the middle before browning too deeply. In other words, you've got to adjust and readjust as you make pancakes.

Finally, you can keep pancakes warm by placing them on a large baking sheet in a 200°F oven for 10 minutes, maybe 15. They won't keep forever. They'll start to toughen and dry out. So get everyone to the table.

BASIC PANCAKES

Straightforward, sweet, and tender, these pancakes are the gold standard. They also cry out for the standards: butter and maple syrup.

MAKES ABOUT TWELVE 4-INCH PANCAKES

2 cups soft white wheat berries

¼ cup all-purpose flour

¼ cup granulated white sugar

2 teaspoons baking powder

½ teaspoon salt

1½ cups whole or 2 percent milk, at room temperature

2 large eggs, at room temperature

4 tablespoons (½ stick) unsalted butter, melted and cooled to room temperature

1 teaspoon pure vanilla extract

Nonstick cooking spray

1. Put the wheat berries in the large canister; cover and blend at the highest speed to a fine flour, about 1 minute. Add the all-purpose flour, sugar, baking powder, and salt; cover and blend at the highest speed until uniform, about 10 seconds. Add the milk, eggs, melted butter, and vanilla; cover and blend at low speed until smooth, 10 to 20 seconds.

2. Lightly coat a large, nonstick griddle or skillet with nonstick cooking spray and set over medium-low heat for 1 minute. Use ¼ cup of batter per pancake to make several pancakes across the hot surface, spacing them out at least 2 inches apart. Cook until open bubbles dot the wet surface, about 2 minutes. Flip the pancakes with a nonstick-safe spatula and continue cooking until browned, about 1 minute more. Transfer to a platter and make more pancakes, regreasing as necessary.

BUTTERMILK PANCAKES

These pancakes have a slight, tart spark. In fact, we've kept the sugar in the batter low so they'll be a great foil to sweet syrup, jam, or preserves. They're also quite light, not as dense as those in the previous recipe.

MAKES ABOUT TWELVE 4-INCH PANCAKES

1½ cups soft white wheat berries

3 tablespoons all-purpose flour

2 tablespoons granulated sugar

1½ teaspoons baking powder

½ teaspoon baking soda

¼ teaspoon salt

2¼ cups regular buttermilk, at room temperature

1 large egg, plus 1 large egg white, at room temperature

3 tablespoons unsalted butter, melted and cooled to room temperature

1½ teaspoons pure vanilla extract

Nonstick cooking spray

1. Place the wheat berries in the large canister; cover and blend at the highest speed to a fine flour, about 1 minute. Add the all-purpose flour, sugar, baking powder, baking soda, and salt; cover and blend at the highest speed until uniform, about 10 seconds. Add the buttermilk, egg, egg white, melted butter, and vanilla; cover and blend at low speed until smooth, 10 to 20 seconds.

2. Lightly coat a large, nonstick griddle or skillet with nonstick cooking spray and set over medium-low heat for 1 minute. Use ¼ cup of batter per pancake to make several pancakes across the hot surface, spacing them out at least 2 inches apart. Cook until open bubbles dot the wet surface, about 2 minutes. Flip the pancakes with a nonstick-safe spatula and continue cooking until browned, about 1 minute more. Transfer to a platter and continue making more pancakes, regreasing the griddle or skillet as necessary.

SOUR CREAM PANCAKES

Be careful that the melted butter has cooled to room temperature and the other dairy ingredients are also at room temperature. Otherwise, the sour cream can break, turning into little threads in the batter. Make these pancakes some night for dinner. They're terrific alongside a pan-fried ham steak.

MAKES ABOUT TWELVE 4-INCH PANCAKES

1½ cups soft white wheat berries

3 tablespoons granulated white sugar

1½ teaspoons baking soda

½ teaspoon salt

1 cup whole or 2 percent milk, at room temperature

¾ cup regular sour cream, at room temperature

1 large egg, plus 1 large egg white, at room temperature

3 tablespoons unsalted butter, melted and cooled to room temperature

2 teaspoons pure vanilla extract

Nonstick cooking spray

1. Put the wheat berries in the large canister; cover and blend at the highest speed to a fine flour, about 1 minute. Add the sugar, baking soda, and salt; cover and blend at the highest speed until uniform, about 10 seconds. Add the milk, sour cream, egg, egg white, melted butter, and vanilla; cover and blend at low speed until smooth, 10 to 20 seconds.

2. Lightly coat a large, nonstick griddle or skillet with nonstick cooking spray and set over medium-low heat for 1 minute. Use ¼ cup of batter per pancake to make several pancakes across the hot surface, spacing them out at least 2 inches apart. Cook until open bubbles dot the wet surface, about 2 minutes. Flip the pancakes with a nonstick-safe spatula and continue cooking until browned, about 1 minute more. Transfer to a platter and continue making more pancakes, regreasing the griddle or skillet as necessary.

RICOTTA PANCAKES

These are cakier, rather like a cross between the texture of a muffin and that of a standard pancake. • MAKES ABOUT TWELVE 4-INCH PANCAKES

1½ cups soft white wheat berries

½ cup all-purpose flour

1 tablespoon baking powder

½ teaspoon salt

1½ cups whole or 2 percent milk, at room temperature

2 large eggs, at room temperature

½ cup whole-milk ricotta, at room temperature

¼ cup granulated white sugar

1 tablespoon pure vanilla extract

½ teaspoon lemon extract, optional

Nonstick cooking spray

1. Put the wheat berries in the large canister; cover and blend at the highest speed to a fine flour, about 1 minute. Add the all-purpose flour, baking powder, and salt; cover and blend at the highest speed until uniform, about 10 seconds. Add the milk, eggs, ricotta, sugar, vanilla, and lemon extract, if using; cover and blend at low speed until smooth, 10 to 20 seconds.

2. Lightly coat a large, nonstick griddle or skillet with nonstick cooking spray and set over medium-low heat for 1 minute. Use ¼ cup of batter per pancake to make several pancakes across the hot surface, spacing them out at least 2 inches apart. Cook until open bubbles dot the wet surface, about 2 minutes. Flip the pancakes with a nonstick-safe spatula and continue cooking until browned, about 1 minute more. Transfer to a platter and continue making more pancakes, regreasing the griddle or skillet as necessary.

MAPLE-WALNUT PANCAKES

Watch the milk for these sweet, nutty pancakes: you need just enough to get a pourable batter, about like a standard milk shake. You can always add more—but you can't add less. And you'll need to add a little more as the batter sits between batches.

MAKES ABOUT TWELVE 4-INCH PANCAKES

1 cup soft white wheat berries

1½ teaspoons baking powder

½ teaspoon salt

1 cup whole or 2 percent milk, plus more as needed

½ cup chopped walnuts

¼ cup maple syrup, preferably grade B or 2

1 large egg, at room temperature

2 tablespoons quick-cooking oats

Nonstick cooking spray

1. Place the wheat berries in the large canister; cover and blend at the highest speed to a fine flour, about 1 minute. Add the baking powder and salt; cover and blend until uniform, about 10 seconds. Add the milk, walnuts, maple syrup, egg, and oats. Cover and blend at low speed to further chop the nuts without grinding them into a paste. Add a little more milk to make the batter pourable, if necessary, but not so thin that it spreads quickly.

(continued)

2. Lightly coat a large, nonstick griddle or skillet with nonstick cooking spray and set over medium-low heat for 1 minute. Use a *scant* ¼ cup of batter per pancake to make several pancakes across the hot surface, spacing them out at least 2 inches apart. Cook until open bubbles dot the wet surface, about 2 minutes. Flip the pancakes with a non-stick-safe spatula and continue cooking until browned, about 1 minute more. Transfer to a platter and continue making more pancakes, regreasing the griddle or skillet as necessary.

BANANA BREAD PANCAKES

Dense and chewy, these pancakes replicate the texture of our favorite quick bread. They have a tendency to stick, so make sure you grease the griddle or pan well—and then grease it again and again between batches. Note that the batter should be poured out in *scant* ¼-cup increments—about 3 tablespoons or so per pancake. • MAKES ABOUT TWELVE 4-INCH PANCAKES

1½ cups soft white wheat berries

3 tablespoons granulated white sugar

2½ teaspoons baking powder

¼ teaspoon ground cinnamon

¼ teaspoon salt

2 small, ripe bananas, peeled and cut into chunks

1 cup whole or 2 percent milk, at room temperature

2 large eggs, at room temperature

3 tablespoons unsalted butter, melted and cooled to room temperature

1 teaspoon pure vanilla extract

Nonstick cooking spray

1. Put the wheat berries in the large canister; cover and blend at the highest speed to a fine flour, about 1 minute. Add the sugar, baking powder, cinnamon, and salt; cover and blend at the highest speed until uniform, about 10 seconds. Add the bananas, milk, eggs, melted butter, and vanilla; cover and blend at low speed until smooth, 10 to 20 seconds.

2. Lightly coat a large, nonstick griddle or skillet with nonstick cooking spray and set over medium-low heat for 1 minute. Use a *scant* ¼ cup of batter per pancake to make several pancakes across the hot surface, spacing them out at least 2 inches apart. Cook until open bubbles dot the wet surface, about 2 minutes. Flip the pancakes with a non-stick-safe spatula and continue cooking until browned, about 1 minute more. Transfer to a platter and continue making more pancakes, regreasing the griddle or skillet after each batch.

JAM PANCAKES

We've put the jam right in the batter for a denser, chewier texture. These are quite sweet—and so best made a little smaller—like old-fashioned silver dollar pancakes. Use about 2 tablespoons of batter per pancake. Of course, we suggest raspberry jam because we're partial to it; but you could use any flavor you like, just not preserves or jelly. MAKES ABOUT SIXTEEN 2-INCH PANCAKES

¾ cup soft white wheat berries

2 tablespoons all-purpose flour

1½ teaspoons baking powder

¼ teaspoon salt

⅔ cup whole or 2 percent milk, at room temperature

¼ cup seedless raspberry jam

2 tablespoons canola oil

1 large egg, at room temperature

Nonstick cooking spray

1. Put the wheat berries in the large canister; cover and blend at the highest speed to a fine flour, about 1 minute. Add the flour, baking powder, and salt; cover and blend at the highest speed until uniform, about 10 seconds. Add the milk, jam, oil, and egg; cover and blend at low speed until smooth, 10 to 20 seconds.

2. Lightly coat a large, nonstick griddle or skillet with nonstick cooking spray and set over medium-low heat for 1 minute. Use 2 tablespoons of batter per pancake to make many small pancakes across the hot surface, spacing them out at least 1 inch apart. Cook until open bubbles dot the wet surface, about 1½ minutes. Flip the pancakes with a nonstick-safe spatula and continue cooking until browned, about 30 seconds more. Transfer to a platter and continue making more pancakes, regreasing the griddle or skillet as necessary.

CHOCOLATE PANCAKES

Think of these as brownies turned into pancakes. Need we say more? • MAKES ABOUT TWELVE 4-INCH PANCAKES

1¼ cups soft white wheat berries

½ cup unsweetened cocoa powder

½ cup granulated white sugar

¼ cup all-purpose flour

1 teaspoon baking powder

1 teaspoon salt

½ teaspoon baking soda

1½ cups whole or 2 percent milk, at room temperature

4 tablespoons (½ stick) unsalted butter, melted and cooled to room temperature

2 large eggs, at room temperature

1 teaspoon pure vanilla extract

Nonstick cooking spray

1. Put the wheat berries in the large canister; cover and blend at the highest speed to a fine flour, about 1 minute. Add the cocoa powder, sugar, all-purpose flour, baking powder, salt, and baking soda; cover and blend at the highest speed until uniform, about 10 seconds. Add the milk, melted butter, eggs, and vanilla; cover and blend at low speed until smooth, 10 to 20 seconds.

2. Lightly coat a large, nonstick griddle or skillet with nonstick cooking spray and set over medium-low heat for 1 minute. Use ¼ cup of batter per pancake to make several pancakes across the hot surface, spacing them out at least 2 inches apart. Cook until open bubbles form at the edge of each pancake, a little less than 2 minutes. Flip the pancakes with a nonstick-safe spatula and continue cooking until browned, about 1 minute more. Transfer to a platter and continue making more pancakes, regreasing the griddle or skillet as necessary.

CRANBERRY PANCAKES

Watch out: they're pink! But by grinding the cranberries a bit into the batter, we can get their tart zip in every bite. We add a little quick cranberry jam for a perfect finish.

MAKES ABOUT TWELVE 4-INCH PANCAKES

1 cup fresh or frozen cranberries (do not thaw)

5 tablespoons granulated white sugar

1 tablespoon light corn syrup

¾ cup plus 2 tablespoons soft white wheat berries

2 tablespoons yellow cornmeal

1 teaspoon baking powder

¼ teaspoon freshly grated nutmeg or ⅛ teaspoon ground nutmeg

¼ teaspoon salt

¾ cup whole or 2 percent milk

1 large egg

3 tablespoons canola oil

1 teaspoon pure vanilla extract

Nonstick cooking spray

Confectioners' sugar, for garnish

1. Mix ½ cup cranberries, 3 tablespoons of the granulated white sugar, and the corn syrup in a medium saucepan set over medium heat. Cook, stirring occasionally, until the cranberries have softened and the liquid is bubbling, about 3 minutes. Cover and set aside on the back of the stove to keep warm while you make the pancakes.

2. Put the wheat berries in the large canister; cover and blend at the highest speed to a fine flour, about 1 minute. Add the remaining 2 tablespoons granulated white sugar, along with the cornmeal, baking powder, nutmeg, and salt. Cover and blend at the highest speed until uniform, about 10 seconds. Add the milk, egg, oil, and vanilla; cover and blend at low speed until smooth, 10 to 20 seconds. Add the remaining ½ cup cranberries, cover, and pulse just to chop and combine.

3. Lightly coat a large, nonstick griddle or skillet with nonstick cooking spray and set over medium-low heat for 1 minute. Use ¼ cup of batter per pancake to make several pancakes across the hot surface, spacing them out at least 2 inches apart. Cook until open bubbles dot the wet surface, about 2 minutes. Flip the pancakes with a nonstick-safe spatula and continue cooking until browned, about 1 minute more. Transfer to a platter and continue making more pancakes, regreasing the griddle or skillet as necessary. Top each serving with a little of the warm cranberry jam and sprinkle with confectioners' sugar, if desired.

LEMON-POPPY SEED PANCAKES

We've added a hefty pour of poppy seeds to this batter to get their slightly earthy flavor throughout—a great balance to the sour lemon in the sweet pancakes. In fact, by grinding those poppy seeds just slightly in the blender, we'll get more of their characteristic flavor in every bite. • MAKES TWELVE 4-INCH PANCAKES

1⅔ cups soft white wheat berries

1 tablespoon granulated white sugar

1 tablespoon baking powder

¼ teaspoon salt

1 cup whole or 2 percent milk, at room temperature

½ cup plain whole-milk Greek yogurt, at room temperature

2 large eggs, at room temperature

1½ tablespoons unsalted butter, melted and cooled to room temperature

1 teaspoon pure vanilla extract

2 tablespoons poppy seeds

1 tablespoon lemon juice

1 teaspoon finely grated lemon zest

½ teaspoon lemon extract

Nonstick cooking spray

1. Put the wheat berries in the large canister; cover and blend at the highest speed to a fine flour, about 1 minute. Add the sugar, baking powder, and salt; cover and blend at the highest speed until uniform, about 10 seconds. Add the milk, yogurt, eggs, melted butter, and vanilla; cover and blend at low speed until smooth, 10 to 20 seconds. Add the poppy seeds, lemon juice, lemon zest, and lemon

extract; cover and blend at low speed just to combine, no more than 5 seconds (to keep the poppy seeds from being entirely ground up).

2. Lightly coat a large, nonstick griddle or skillet with nonstick cooking spray and set over medium-low heat for 1 minute. Use ¼ cup of batter per pancake to make several pancakes across the hot surface, spacing them out at least 2 inches apart. Cook until open bubbles dot the wet surface, about 2 minutes. Flip the pancakes with a nonstick-safe spatula and continue cooking until browned, about 1 minute more. Transfer to a platter and continue making more pancakes, regreasing the griddle or skillet as necessary between each batch.

NOTE: Consider serving these with fruit preserves and sweetened sour cream (whisk 1½ tablespoons confectioners' sugar into each cup of sour cream).

BUCKWHEAT PANCAKES

Provided you buy raw, certified gluten-free buckwheat groats, these are indeed gluten-free pancakes. They're light but definitely chewy, with a slight herbal flavor from the buckwheat. Do not use toasted or parboiled buckwheat groats, sometimes called "kasha." The flavor will become too pronounced. If you're not concerned about gluten issues, you can soften the flavor a bit by using 1 cup buckwheat groats and ½ cup soft white wheat berries. • MAKES ABOUT TWELVE 4-INCH PANCAKES

(continued)

1½ cups raw, untoasted buckwheat groats (see Note)

1½ teaspoons baking powder

1½ teaspoons baking soda

¼ teaspoon salt

2 cups regular buttermilk

¼ cup canola oil

1½ tablespoons honey

1 large egg, plus 1 large egg white

1 teaspoon pure vanilla extract

Nonstick cooking spray

1. Put the buckwheat groats in the large canister; cover and blend at the highest speed to a fine flour, about 1 minute. Add the baking powder, baking soda, and salt; cover and blend at the highest speed until uniform, about 10 seconds. Add the buttermilk, oil, honey, egg, egg white, and vanilla; cover and blend at low speed until smooth, 10 to 20 seconds.

2. Lightly coat a large, nonstick griddle or skillet with nonstick cooking spray and set over medium-low heat for 1 minute. Use ¼ cup batter per pancake to make several pancakes across the hot surface, spacing them out at least 2 inches apart. Cook until open bubbles dot the wet surface, about 2 minutes. Flip the pancakes with a nonstick-safe spatula and continue cooking until browned, less than 1 minute more. Transfer to a platter and continue making more pancakes, regreasing the griddle or skillet as necessary between each batch.

NOTE: Despite its name, buckwheat is not a wheat. It's a grass closely related to rhubarb. It has a starch content rather similar to rice—and thus its sticky nature when cooked without being toasted.

OAT AND HONEY PANCAKES

If you like oatmeal, you've come to the right place . . . for pancakes! We grind steel-cut oats into the batter for the best flavor and that characteristic texture of baked goods made with oats. We find these irresistible with lots of butter and syrup. • MAKES ABOUT TWELVE 4-INCH PANCAKES

1½ cups steel-cut oats

½ cup soft white wheat berries

1½ teaspoons baking powder

½ teaspoon ground cinnamon

¼ teaspoon salt

1¼ cups regular buttermilk

2 tablespoons canola oil

2 tablespoons honey

1 large egg

Nonstick cooking spray

Water, as needed

1. Place the steel-cut oats and wheat berries in the large canister; cover and blend at the highest speed to a fine flour, about 1 minute. Add the baking powder, cinnamon, and salt; cover and blend at the highest speed until uniform, about 10 seconds. Add the buttermilk, oil, honey, and egg; cover and blend at low speed until smooth, 10 to 20 seconds.

2. Lightly coat a large, nonstick griddle or skillet with nonstick cooking spray and set over medium-low heat for 1 minute. Use a *scant* ¼ cup of batter per pancake to make several across the hot surface, spacing them out at least 2 inches apart. Cook until open bubbles dot the wet surface, about 2 minutes. Flip the pancakes with a nonstick-safe spatula

and continue cooking until browned, about 1 minute more. Transfer to a platter and continue making more pancakes, stirring water into the batter in 1-tablespoon increments as necessary to keep the batter pourable. Also regrease the griddle or skillet as necessary between batches.

QUINOA PANCAKES

These are dense! In fact, the batter won't yield many bubbles in the griddle or skillet—and the pancakes will cook pretty quickly. Some quinoa is not rinsed and so may contain a bitter, natural chemical that adheres to each grain. Read the package you've got in hand or ask questions if you've bought it at a health-food store. If you're in doubt, rinse the grains with cold water in a fine-mesh sieve set in the sink, stirring them repeatedly to get them as clean as possible. Dry thoroughly before continuing with this recipe. • MAKES ABOUT TWELVE 4-INCH PANCAKES

1½ cups white or blond quinoa, rinsed if necessary

½ cup all-purpose flour

2 tablespoons packed light brown sugar

1½ teaspoons baking powder

½ teaspoon ground cinnamon

½ teaspoon salt

1½ cups whole milk (see Note)

2 large eggs

3 tablespoons canola oil

2 teaspoons pure vanilla extract

Nonstick cooking spray

1. Put the quinoa in the large canister; cover and blend at the highest speed to a fine flour, about 1 minute. Add the all-purpose flour, sugar, baking powder, cinnamon, and salt; cover and blend at the highest speed until uniform, about 10 seconds. Add the milk, eggs, oil, and vanilla; cover and blend at low speed until smooth, 10 to 20 seconds.

2. Lightly coat a large, nonstick griddle or skillet with nonstick cooking spray and set over medium-low heat for 1 minute. Use ¼ cup of batter per pancake to make several pancakes across the hot surface, spacing them out at least 2 inches apart. Cook until lightly browned with very few bubbles, about 1 minute. Flip the pancakes with a nonstick-safe spatula and continue cooking until browned, no more than 1 minute longer. Transfer to a platter and continue making more pancakes, regreasing the griddle or skillet as necessary between each batch.

NOTE: Because of the way quinoa saps the moisture out of a batter, do not use low-fat milk.

ROLLED PANCAKES

Here are some very thin pancakes, sort of a halfway point between pancakes and crepes. We developed them so they could be rolled around the jam filling before serving. You'll need a nonstick, 8-inch skillet. They'll spread quite a bit, about like a crepe. You'll only be able to make one at a time, so just stack them up on a plate and soldier on. They also make a great dessert for friends on a weekend evening. • MAKES 8 FILLED PANCAKES

(continued)

1 cup soft white wheat berries

2 large eggs

½ cup plain whole-milk yogurt
(do not use Greek-style yogurt)

½ cup whole or 2 percent milk

1 teaspoon pure vanilla extract

¼ teaspoon salt

2 tablespoons water, as needed

Nonstick cooking spray

About ½ cup jam (of any sort)

Confectioners' sugar, for garnish

1. Put the wheat berries in the large canister; cover and blend at the highest speed to a fine flour, about 1 minute. Add the eggs, yogurt, milk, vanilla, and salt; cover and blend at the highest speed until smooth, about 20 seconds. The batter should be quite thin; add water in ½-tablespoon increments as necessary to make sure the batter is distinctly pourable, not as thick as a traditional pancake batter.

2. Lightly coat a nonstick, 8-inch skillet with nonstick cooking spray and set over medium-low heat for 1 minute. Use ¼ cup of batter to make 1 pancake. Tip and tilt the skillet so that the batter spreads out into a 5- to 6-inch diameter pancake. Cook until many bubbles dot its surface, about 1 minute. Flip the pancake with a nonstick-safe spatula and continue cooking just until set, about 30 seconds more, maybe less. Transfer to a platter and continue making more pancakes, regreasing the skillet between each batch. When done, spread each pancake with 1 tablespoon of the jam and roll up to serve. Dust with confectioners' sugar as a garnish, if desired.

NOTE: Yes, grease even a nonstick skillet. These pancakes can stick like mad.

GLUTEN-FREE PANCAKES

Just because you need to or want to do without certain things doesn't mean you can't have a terrific pancake. We suggest strawberry preserves with these—a great match to the delicate corn flavor in the cakes. • MAKES ABOUT TWELVE 4-INCH PANCAKES

1 cup yellow cornmeal

⅔ cup certified gluten-free old-fashioned rolled oats (do not use quick-cooking or steel-cut)

½ cup long-grain white rice, such as white basmati rice

½ cup millet grains (see Note)

¼ cup granulated white sugar

2 teaspoons baking powder

1 teaspoon baking soda

¼ teaspoon salt

1½ cups regular buttermilk

¼ cup canola or vegetable oil

2 teaspoons pure vanilla extract

Nonstick cooking spray

1. Put the cornmeal, oats, rice, and millet in the large canister; cover and blend at the highest speed to a fine flour, about 1 minute. Add the sugar, baking powder, baking soda, and salt; cover and blend at the highest speed until uniform, about 10 seconds. Add the buttermilk, oil, and vanilla; cover and blend at low speed until smooth, about 20 seconds.

2. Lightly coat a large, nonstick griddle or skillet with nonstick cooking spray and set over medium-low heat for 1 minute. Use ¼ cup of batter per pancake to make several pancakes across the hot surface, spacing them out at least 2 inches apart. Cook until open bubbles dot the wet surface, about 2 minutes.

Flip the pancakes with a nonstick-safe spatula and continue cooking until browned, about 1 minute more. Transfer to a platter and continue making more pancakes, regreasing the griddle or skillet as necessary between each batch.

NOTE: Millet goes rancid very quickly. Smell your packaging to make sure it doesn't have an acrid aroma. Store millet tightly sealed in the freezer for a couple of months. And work with millet in the sink. If you spill those tiny grains, you will never stop vacuuming your kitchen. Trust us.

BUTTERMILK DUTCH BABY

Although lots of us know about apple Dutch babies, here's the original: a single, thick, cakey pancake in a skillet. Nonstick cookware is safe up to 400°F, but not much above that, so we recommend using a well-seasoned, 10-inch, cast-iron skillet. If you use a standard skillet, you'll need to add 3 tablespoons of butter in step 2, and you'll need to watch the baking process, adding some extra time since a shiny surface will retain less heat than a black one. Have plenty of butter and jam ready for the table. You'll get four servings out of this one if it's the only thing for breakfast, or six servings if you've got eggs and bacon on the side. • MAKES ONE 10-INCH PANCAKE

2 tablespoons unsalted butter

½ cup soft white wheat berries

3 tablespoons granulated white sugar

2 tablespoons all-purpose flour

½ teaspoon baking powder

½ teaspoon baking soda

½ teaspoon salt

½ cup regular buttermilk, at room temperature

2 large eggs, at room temperature

1 teaspoon pure vanilla extract

1 tablespoon unsalted butter, melted and cooled to room temperature

1. Position the rack in the center of the oven; heat the oven to 400°F.

2. Once the oven has reached the proper temperature, put the 2 tablespoons butter in a 10-inch oven-safe, cast-iron skillet and set in the heated oven for 10 minutes.

3. Meanwhile, put the wheat berries in the large canister; cover and blend at the highest speed to a fine flour, about 1 minute. Add the sugar, all-purpose flour, baking powder, baking soda, and salt; cover and blend at the highest speed until uniform, about 10 seconds. Add the buttermilk, eggs, vanilla, and the melted butter; cover and blend at low speed until smooth, 10 to 20 seconds.

4. Using a hot pad or oven mitts to handle the skillet, swirl the now melted butter around the inside of the skillet to coat. Pour in the batter and bake until puffed and set, about 20 minutes. Cool the Dutch baby on a wire rack for 5 minutes before slicing into quarters to serve.

OVEN-BAKED PANCAKE CAKE

This one is pure whimsy. Basically, it's a coffee cake made from pancake batter. It will be soft and moist at its center—and better with apricot or strawberry preserves. Consider it a brunch dish or perhaps a late-night snack after a movie. • MAKES ONE 9 X 13-INCH CAKE

Nonstick cooking spray

2 cups soft white wheat berries

2 tablespoons granulated white sugar

1 tablespoon baking powder

½ teaspoon salt

1½ cups whole milk

6 tablespoons canola oil

2 large eggs

1 teaspoon pure vanilla extract

1. Position the rack in the center of the oven; heat the oven to 350°F. Lightly coat the inside of a 9 x 13-inch baking pan with nonstick cooking spray.

2. Put the wheat berries in the large canister; cover and blend at the highest speed to a fine flour, about 1 minute. Add the sugar, baking powder, and salt; cover and blend at the highest speed until uniform, about 10 seconds. Add the milk, oil, eggs, and vanilla; cover and blend at low speed until smooth, 10 to 20 seconds. Pour the batter into the prepared pan.

3. Bake until browned, until a toothpick or cake tester inserted into the middle of the cake comes out clean, 18 to 20 minutes. Cool on a wire rack for 5 minutes before slicing into squares or rectangles to serve.

APPLE DUTCH BABY

Use moderately sweet baking apples for the best texture and flavor. They should break down a bit and become saucy just at their sides. • MAKES ONE 10-INCH PANCAKE; SERVES 4

¾ cup soft white wheat berries

¾ cup whole milk

3 large eggs

1 teaspoon pure vanilla extract

¼ teaspoon salt

3 tablespoons unsalted butter

2 medium, sweet apples, such as Gala apples, peeled, cored, and thinly sliced

1 tablespoon packed light brown sugar

½ teaspoon ground cinnamon

1. Position the rack in the center of the oven; heat the oven to 400°F.

2. Put the wheat berries in the large canister; cover and blend at the highest speed to a fine flour, about 1 minute. Add the milk, eggs, vanilla, and salt; cover and blend at low speed until smooth, about 20 seconds. Set aside.

3. Melt the butter in a 10-inch oven-safe cast-iron skillet set over medium heat. Add the apple slices and cook, stirring often, until softened, about 5 minutes. Sprinkle the sugar and cinnamon over the slices; cook until the sauce is bubbling, stirring occasionally.

4. Arrange the apple slices in an even layer. Pour the batter in the canister evenly over the apples. Bake until set, about 20 minutes. Cool on a wire rack for 5 minutes before turning upside down onto a serving platter and slicing into wedges to serve.

WAFFLES

NEXT TO THE PROPER WAY TO LOAD A DISHWASHER, THE PROPER WAY TO COOK A WAFFLE IS THE LEADING CAUSE OF DIVORCE IN NORTH AMERICA. (STATISTICS FORTHCOMING. SURELY.)

Some people like their waffles soft, a little spongy at their centers. Then there are the people who are right. They like them very crisp, about like shingles. Fortunately, we can satisfy both groups with these recipes. If you leave a waffle in the iron for at least half the duration of a second cycle, you can dry it out a bit and avoid arbitration.

If you've got crowds, don't double these recipes. You'll overwhelm the blender. Instead, make a second batch when you're done with the first. Let's face it: making waffle batter in a turbo blender is so easy, you won't find it a big deal. Measure out the ingredients for the second batch while the first cooks to make things speedier.

YIELDS

Different size waffle irons will produce different yields. We tested every one of these waffles in a 6⅝-inch (or 17-centimeter) diameter waffle

maker. It's listed as a "Belgian" waffle maker because, well, they all are these days. But it doesn't have deep pockets the way we'd expect in a Belgian waffle maker. If your waffle maker is different from ours, you'll get a different yield. Familiarize yourself with the instructions for your particular machine. It will help you best understand the timing and batter requirements to make a successful batch.

IMPERFECT TIMING

Waffles are easy to keep warm: line them up on a baking sheet and hold in a 200°F oven for 15 minutes or so. And once made, waffles are a snap to freeze. Just cool them on a wire rack to room temperature, seal in plastic wrap, and store in the freezer for up to 3 months. You can reheat them straight out of the freezer on a baking sheet in a 300°F oven for 10 or 15 minutes.

BASIC WAFFLES

There's a range for the quantity of milk here because you might grind the wheat berries a little more finely than we do or your grains might have a little less moisture content than ours. In the end, you want a batter that's a little thicker than pancake batter but still pourable. • MAKES 6 TO 8 MEDIUM WAFFLES

2 cups soft white wheat berries

3 tablespoons granulated white sugar

1 teaspoon baking powder

½ teaspoon salt

1¾ cups whole or 2 percent milk, plus more as necessary

3 large eggs, at room temperature

4 tablespoons (½ stick) unsalted butter, melted and cooled to room temperature

1 teaspoon pure vanilla extract

Nonstick cooking spray

1. Put the wheat berries in the large canister; cover and blend at the highest speed to a fine flour, about 1 minute. Add the sugar, baking powder, and salt; cover and blend at the highest speed until uniform, about 10 seconds. Add the milk, eggs, butter, and vanilla; cover and blend at low speed until smooth, 10 to 20 seconds. Add a little extra milk if you find that the batter is so thick you can't pour it.

2. Lightly coat the plates of a waffle iron with nonstick cooking spray. Heat the iron and make the waffles according to the manufacturer's instructions.

BUTTERMILK WAFFLES

Buttermilk gives these waffles more rise and so they're better suited to Belgian-style waffle makers. As such, they're great with preserves or an all-fruit spread, rather than syrup.
MAKES 6 TO 8 MEDIUM WAFFLES

2 cups soft white wheat berries

3 tablespoons granulated white sugar

1 teaspoon baking powder

½ teaspoon baking soda

½ teaspoon salt

2 cups regular buttermilk, at room temperature

2 large eggs, at room temperature

4 tablespoons (½ stick) unsalted butter, melted and cooled to room temperature

1 teaspoon pure vanilla extract

Nonstick cooking spray

1. Put the wheat berries in the large canister; cover and blend at the highest speed to a fine flour, about 1 minute. Add the sugar, baking powder, baking soda, and salt; cover and blend at the highest speed until uniform, about 10 seconds. Add the buttermilk, eggs, melted butter, and vanilla; cover and blend at low speed until smooth, 10 to 20 seconds.

2. Lightly coat the plates of a waffle iron with nonstick cooking spray. Heat the iron and make the waffles according to the manufacturer's instructions.

MALT WAFFLES

Malt adds rich, earthy notes to these waffles. It also thickens the batter considerably. Make sure you use malted milk powder, not diastatic malt powder, a specialty, bread-making product. • MAKES 6 TO 8 MEDIUM WAFFLES

1½ cups soft white wheat berries

⅓ cup yellow cornmeal

¼ cup granulated white sugar

3 tablespoons malted milk powder

1 teaspoon baking powder

½ teaspoon salt

1¼ cups whole or 2 percent milk, at room temperature

2 large eggs, at room temperature

4 tablespoons (½ stick) unsalted butter, melted and cooled to room temperature

1 teaspoon pure vanilla extract

Nonstick cooking spray

1. Put the wheat berries in the large canister; cover and blend at the highest speed to a fine flour, about 1 minutes. Add the cornmeal, sugar, malted milk powder, baking powder, and salt; cover and blend at the highest speed until uniform, about 10 seconds. Add the milk, eggs, melted butter, and vanilla; cover and blend at low speed until smooth, 10 to 20 seconds. Remove the canister from the housing and set aside at room temperature for 10 to 15 minutes to allow the batter to thicken somewhat.

2. Lightly coat the plates of a waffle iron with nonstick cooking spray. Heat the iron and make the waffles according to the manufacturer's instructions.

SWEET POTATO WAFFLES

These waffles pair well with sliced apples cooked in a little butter with brown sugar and cinnamon—or just some apple butter. The waffles will burn quite easily because of the sugar content of the sweet potatoes. Set your iron on a slightly lower setting and watch carefully. • MAKES ABOUT SIX 8-INCH WAFFLES

1¼ cups soft white wheat berries

¼ cup all-purpose flour

1 teaspoon baking powder

½ teaspoon baking soda

½ teaspoon ground cinnamon

½ teaspoon salt

¼ teaspoon freshly grated nutmeg

1 cup canned yams in heavy syrup, drained

1 cup regular buttermilk, at room temperature

¼ cup packed light brown sugar

4 tablespoons (½ stick) unsalted butter, melted and cooled to room temperature

1 large egg, at room temperature

Nonstick cooking spray

1. Put the wheat berries in the large canister; cover and blend at the highest speed to a fine flour, about 1 minute. Add the all-purpose flour, baking powder, baking soda, cinnamon, salt, and nutmeg; cover and blend at the highest speed until uniform, about 10 seconds. Add the yams, buttermilk, sugar, melted butter, and egg; cover and blend at low speed until smooth, about 20 seconds.

2. Lightly coat the plates of a waffle iron with nonstick cooking spray. Heat the iron and make the waffles according to the manufacturer's instructions.

YEAST-RAISED WAFFLES

These are the lightest, most tender waffles in the chapter. The eggs need to be at room temperature so they don't shock the yeast. But here's a bit of good news: you can make this batter the night before and let it rise in the refrigerator. • MAKES 6 TO 8 MEDIUM WAFFLES

2 cups soft white wheat berries

2 cups whole or 2 percent milk

8 tablespoons (1 stick) unsalted butter, softened to room temperature

¼ cup all-purpose flour

3 tablespoons granulated white sugar

2 teaspoons instant yeast (see Note)

1 teaspoon salt

2 large eggs, at room temperature

¼ teaspoon baking soda

Nonstick cooking spray

1. Put the wheat berries in the large canister; cover and blend at the highest speed to a fine flour, about 1 minute. Add the milk, butter, flour, sugar, yeast, and salt; cover and blend at the highest speed just until smooth but quite thick, about 10 seconds. Keep the canister covered and set aside at room temperature until doubled in bulk, about 1½ hours—or store in the refrigerator overnight, or for up to 15 hours.

2. Add the eggs and baking soda to the canister. Cover and blend at low speed, stopping the blender repeatedly to scrape down the inside of the canister, or using the tamper, if available, until smooth, about 20 seconds.

3. Lightly coat the plates of a waffle iron with nonstick cooking spray. Heat the iron and make the waffles according to the manufacturer's instructions.

NOTE: This recipe calls for instant yeast, not active dry yeast. Instant yeast is a specialty product found in large supermarkets and from many online suppliers. It's a foolproof product that allows you to make this batter the night before and finish off the waffles the next morning.

BANANA-PECAN WAFFLES

We added both cinnamon and nutmeg to these waffles to give them an autumnal flare. The pecans add a little fat to the batter along with their earthy, sweet flavor. • MAKES 6 TO 8 MEDIUM WAFFLES

1½ cups soft white wheat berries

2 teaspoons baking powder

½ teaspoon salt

¼ teaspoon ground cinnamon

¼ teaspoon freshly grated nutmeg

2 small, very ripe bananas, peeled and cut into chunks

¾ cup regular sour cream, at room temperature

5 tablespoons (½ stick plus 1 tablespoon) unsalted butter, melted and cooled to room temperature

2 large eggs, at room temperature

1 teaspoon pure vanilla extract

½ cup chopped pecans

Nonstick cooking spray

(continued)

1. Put the wheat berries in the large canister; cover and blend at the highest speed to a fine flour, about 1 minute. Add the baking powder, salt, cinnamon, and nutmeg; cover and blend at the highest speed until uniform, about 10 seconds.

2. Add the bananas, sour cream, melted butter, eggs, and vanilla; cover and blend at low speed until smooth, about 20 seconds. Add the pecans and pulse a few times, just enough to combine and without grinding the nuts too much.

3. Lightly coat the plates of a waffle iron with nonstick cooking spray. Heat the iron and make the waffles according to the manufacturer's instructions.

APPLE BUTTER WAFFLES

Here's a rather unusual waffle. It's not crisp. In fact, it won't ever get crisp. And it burns easily, so use a low setting on your waffle iron until you get the hang of it. That said, these waffles are sweet and delicate. Serve them with butter and even more apple butter.

MAKES 6 TO 8 WAFFLES

1½ cups soft white wheat berries

2 teaspoons baking powder

½ teaspoon ground cinnamon

½ teaspoon salt

¾ cup apple butter

¾ cup whole or 2 percent milk

2 large eggs

¼ cup packed light brown sugar

Nonstick cooking spray

1. Put the wheat berries in the large canister; cover and blend at the highest speed to a fine flour, about 1 minute. Add the baking powder, cinnamon, and salt; cover and blend at the highest speed until uniform, about 10 seconds. Add the apple butter, milk, eggs, and brown sugar; cover and blend at low speed until smooth, 10 to 20 seconds.

2. Lightly coat the plates of a waffle iron with nonstick cooking spray. Heat the iron and make the waffles according to the manufacturer's instructions.

PEANUT BUTTER WAFFLES

Some of us grew up putting peanut butter on waffles instead of butter. Some of us still do. So some of us developed a recipe so we don't have to bring the jar to the table. Despite what you might think, these are best with maple syrup, not jam. • MAKES 6 TO 8 MEDIUM WAFFLES

1½ cups soft white wheat berries

2 tablespoons granulated white sugar

1 tablespoon baking powder

¼ teaspoon salt, optional

1¼ cups whole or 2 percent milk

½ cup peanut butter (of any sort)

6 tablespoons canola oil

2 large eggs

2 teaspoons pure vanilla extract

Nonstick cooking spray

1. Put the wheat berries in the large canister; cover and blend at the highest speed to a fine flour, about 1 minute. Add the sugar, baking powder, and salt, if using; cover and blend at the highest speed until uniform, about 10 seconds. Add the milk, peanut butter, oil, eggs, and vanilla; cover and blend at low speed until smooth, about 20 seconds.

2. Lightly coat the plates of a waffle iron with nonstick cooking spray. Heat the iron and make the waffles according to the manufacturer's instructions.

BUCKWHEAT WAFFLES

These are chewy but light waffles, with sophisticated, herbaceous notes among all the sweetness. The sour cream brings the flavors into better balance. Try these as a nice morning pick-me-up or brunch treat. MAKES 6 TO 8 MEDIUM WAFFLES

1½ cups soft white wheat berries

1 cup untoasted buckwheat groats (see Note)

¼ cup granulated white sugar

1 tablespoon baking powder

1 teaspoon salt

1½ cups regular milk, at room temperature

½ cup regular sour cream, at room temperature

6 tablespoons (¾ stick) unsalted butter, melted and cooled to room temperature

1 teaspoon pure vanilla extract

Nonstick cooking spray

1. Put the wheat berries and buckwheat groats in the large canister; cover and blend at the highest speed to a fine flour, about 1 minute. Add the sugar, baking powder, and salt; cover and blend at the highest speed until uniform, about 10 seconds. Add the milk, sour cream, melted butter, and vanilla; cover and blend at low speed until smooth, 10 to 20 seconds.

2. Lightly coat the plates of a waffle iron with nonstick cooking spray. Heat the iron and make the waffles according to the manufacturer's instructions.

NOTE: Do not use toasted buckwheat, sometimes called "kasha." The flavor will be too assertive.

GLUTEN-FREE RICE AND OAT WAFFLES

Here's our first gluten-free waffle, a mixture of rice and oats. For a more assertive flavor, substitute a toasted nut oil for the canola or vegetable oil. · MAKES 6 TO 8 MEDIUM WAFFLES

1½ cups raw long-grain white rice

1½ cups certified gluten-free old-fashioned rolled oats

2 teaspoons baking powder

1 teaspoon baking soda

1 teaspoon granulated white sugar

½ teaspoon salt

1½ cups whole or 2 percent milk

2 large eggs

¼ cup canola or vegetable oil

1 teaspoon pure vanilla extract

Nonstick cooking spray

1. Put the rice in the large canister; cover and blend at the highest speed until it has the texture of flour, about 1 minute. Add the oats, baking powder, baking soda, sugar, and salt; cover and blend at the highest speed until the oats are coarsely ground, about 20 seconds. Add the milk, eggs, oil, and vanilla; cover and blend at low speed until smooth, 10 to 20 seconds. Set aside, covered, for 10 minutes at room temperature to allow the batter to set up.

2. Lightly coat the plates of a waffle iron with nonstick cooking spray. Heat the iron and make the waffles according to the manufacturer's instructions.

GLUTEN-FREE BROWN RICE AND CORNMEAL WAFFLES

These waffles have a sweet flavor with a slightly grainy texture. They'll go better with maple syrup than jam. For a more sophisticated flavor palette, substitute ¼ teaspoon almond extract for the vanilla extract.
MAKES 6 TO 8 WAFFLES

1½ cups raw long-grain brown rice

1½ cups yellow cornmeal

¼ cup granulated white sugar

2 teaspoons baking powder

1 teaspoon baking soda

½ teaspoon ground cinnamon

½ teaspoon salt

1¼ cups whole or 2 percent milk

2 large eggs

1 teaspoon pure vanilla extract

Nonstick cooking spray

1. Put the brown rice and cornmeal in the large canister; cover and blend at the highest speed until they have the texture of flour, about 1 minute. Add the sugar, baking powder, baking soda, cinnamon, and salt; cover and blend at the highest speed until uniform, about 10 seconds. Add the milk, eggs, and vanilla; cover and blend at low speed until smooth, 10 to 20 seconds.

2. Lightly coat the plates of a waffle iron with nonstick cooking spray. Heat the iron and make the waffles according to the manufacturer's instructions.

ACKNOWLEDGMENTS

REMEMBER PROGRESSIVE DINNERS, A NEW COURSE AT EVERY HOME? THAT'S WHAT WRITING A COOKBOOK IS LIKE. BY THE END, YOU'RE STUFFED, TIRED, AND VERY HAPPY. HERE'S WHERE WE STOPPED:

- At St. Martin's Press with BJ Berti, Claire Leaden, Marie Estrada, Michelle McMillian, Jan Derevjanik, Michael Storrings, Courtney Littler, and Eric C. Meyer.

- At Writers House with Susan Ginsburg and Stacy Testa

- At Vitamix with Laura Pegg from Falls Communication (so many blenders!)

- At Blendtec with Tim Provost (so many blenders!)

- At Waring with Mary Rodgers and Ilona Gollinger (so many blenders!)

- At OXO with Emily Forest and Gretchen Holt (so many kitchen tools!)

- At Bob's Red Mill with Brendo Gibson and Lori Sobelson (so many wheat berries!)

- At KitchenAid with Jenna Llewellyn at Digitas (so much bakeware!)

- At our house with Eric Medsker (for shots), Caroline Dorn (for props), and Karen O'Dell (for saving our tired feet again)

INDEX

Cape Cod Pie. *See* New England
    Cranberry Pie
Carrot-Raisin Scones, 154–55
Chai Tea Pudding, 15
cheesecake(s), 47–48, 65, 66. *See
    also* cake(s)
    Cherry Vanilla No-Bake, 76
    Mint Chocolate No-Bake, 77
    Orange No-Bake, 78, *79*
    Peanut Butter and Chocolate
        Glaze No-Bake, *80*, 81
    Pineapple, 82
Cherry Vanilla No-Bake
    Cheesecake, 76
Chocolate, Banana, and Peanut
    Butter Ice Box Cake, 71
Chocolate Buttermilk Quick
    Bread, 157
Chocolate Cake Muffins with a
    Vanilla Glaze, *144*, 145
Chocolate Chip Blondies, 96, *97*
Chocolate Chip Scones, *152*, 153
Chocolate-Cream Cheese Pie,
    62, 63
Chocolate Cream Cookies and
    Cream Ice Cream, 37
Chocolate Cream Pie, 52–53
Chocolate Frosting, 118
Chocolate Frozen Yogurt, 28
Chocolate Glaze, *80*, 81, 150, *151*
Chocolate Layer Cake with Old-
    Fashioned Seven Minute
    Frosting, 113–15, *114*
Chocolate Malt Ice Cream, 29
Chocolate Pancakes, 171
Chocolate Panna Cotta, 20
Chocolate Pudding, *6*, 12–13, *13*
Chocolate-Raspberry Brownies,
    96
Chocolate-Raspberry Ice Box
    Cake, 74, *75*
Chocolate Sandwich Cookie
    Crust
    baking tips for, 83
    pies with, 53, 59, *62*, 63, 64
    recipe for, 84–85
Chocolate Syrup Brownies, 93
chocolate, types of, 48, 70

Clafouti, Sweet Cherry, 121, 132,
    133
cobbler(s), 87, 90–91, 120–21
    Blueberry, with Turbo Blender
        Crème Anglaise, 126–28,
        127
    Plum, 125
    Raspberry, with Brown Sugar
        Cake Topping, 128
cocoa powder, 4
Coconut Blondies, 98–99
Coconut Crust, 83, 85
Coconut Custard Pie, 56, *57*
Coconut Pudding, 17
Coffee Panna Cotta, *22*, 23
Corn Muffins, 149
Cracker Jack Ice Cream, 44, *45*
Cranberry Pancakes, 172, *173*
Cranberry Pie, New England,
    129, *130*
Cream Cheese Frosting, 119
cream pie(s), 47–49, *51*. *See also*
    crust(s); pie
    Banana, 53
    Chocolate, 52–53
    Chocolate-Cream Cheese, *62*,
        63
    Coconut Custard, 56, *57*
    Grasshopper, 59
    Key Lime, 58
    Lemon Buttermilk, 56–58, *58*
    Nutella-Ricotta, 64
    PB&J-Cream Cheese, 64
    Pumpkin, 55, 60
    Raspberry, *54*, 55
    set point for, 50
    S'Mores, 60, *61*
    Sweet Potato, 60
    Vanilla, with Turbo Blender
        Whipped Cream, *51*, 52
Crème Anglaise, Turbo Blender,
    126–28, *127*
crisp(s), 87, 90–91, 120–21
    Apple-Pecan, *86*, *122*, 123
    Peach, with Oat-Almond
        Topping, 123–24
    Pear, with Ginger-Walnut
        Topping, 124

crust(s)
    baking tips for, 83
    Chocolate Sandwich Cookie,
        53, 59, *62*, 63, 64, 83, 84
    Coconut, 83, 85
    Graham Cracker, 55, 56, *57*,
        58, 60, *61*, 64, 83, 84
    Salty Pretzel, 83, 85
    store-bought, 50
    Vanilla Cookie, *51*, 52, 53, *54*,
        55, 56, *58*, 64, 83, 84

D

dairy products, recipe tips for, 4
Dark Chocolate Ice Cream, 28
Date-Nut Muffins, 147
Date-Walnut Scones, 154
Devil's Food Sheet Cake with
    Cream Cheese Frosting, 119

F

flouring/greasing pans, 89, 165
Frosting, Chocolate, 118
Frosting, Cream Cheese, 119
Frosting, Seven-Minute, 113–15,
    114
Frozen Yogurt, Chocolate, 28
Frozen Yogurt, Strawberry, 30
Fudgy Brownies, 92

G

gelatin, recipe tips for, 19
Gingerbread, Quick, 156–57
glass baking pans, 89
Glaze, Chocolate, *80*, 81, 150,
    151
Glaze, Lemon, 139
Glaze, Maple, 109
Glaze, Vanilla, *144*, 145
Gluten-Free Blueberry Muffins,
    140–42, **141**
Gluten-Free Brownies, *94*, 95